JERK
MAGNET

A Guide to Demagnetize

by

Dr. Bill Bunn

The names, identifying details, and histories of the patients whose stories appear in this book have been altered and condensed to preserve their privacy and protect their confidentiality.

Library of Congress Cataloging-in-Publication Data

Bunn, Bill.
        Jerk Magnet: A Guide To Demagnetize/Bill Bunn.

        Includes bibliographical references
        ISBN 978-0-9970865-0-8 (trade paper)
        ISBN 978-0-9970865-1-5 (e-book)
1. Self-realization. 2. Self-help (Psychology). 3. Resilience (Personality trait)
4. Autonomy (Psychology)

Cover, interior design, and formatting by Lucas Marc Design

To my Dana, Devon, and Hayden

TABLE OF CONTENTS

CHAPTER ONE

Jerk Magnetism

"So, why do I always go for the wrong guy?" a perplexed twenty-four-year-old woman asked. "It's like I have a sign on me that says 'Jerks of the world unite and date me.'" She is not alone in asking this question. Why do some people have a mysterious unseen force attracting them to Jerk after Jerk? It is amazing how many women begin a relationship thinking they have found Mr. Right only to have him do a 180-degree change to reveal the true Jerk inside. What's that you say? All men are jerks? Well, that's not entirely true and if you think this, you need another book—maybe "Men Haters United." For the rest of you interested in a better understanding of Jerk Magnetism and to learn the step-by-step process to demagnetize, this book is for you.

Before you can demagnetize, you first need to understand the forces that create Jerk Magnetism. Let's begin with an example of my experience with a person I'll call Jessica:

I received a call from a mother who was in desperate need of help for Jessica, her twenty-four-year-old daughter. "She has always gone for jerks and now she is engaged to a jerk and needs help to escape." She went on to explain that her daughter, for whatever reason, has never felt good about herself and beginning in junior high had a string of mean boyfriends. When she was seven years old, one of her friends told her she looked too pretty to go to school. She came home, changed her clothes, messed up her hair and returned to school. She had always been this way. She was a pleaser. As the oldest of four children, she was the peacemaker. Her mother recounted several of her early boyfriends and how they would boss her around. They would tell her what and what not to wear. She even developed an eating disorder at age fifteen when her boyfriend told her she was too fat. "She was a hundred pounds, for Pete's sake," her mother exclaimed.

Her most recent boyfriend/fiancé had started out "perfect." He was handsome, kind, and wanted to be with Jessica "all the time." She was flattered by his jealousy of others including her roommates. If she would go out with her girlfriends, he would show up unannounced and somehow always knew where she was. As time went on, he began to dictate whom she could and could not see. He began trying to separate Jessica from her family. When Jessica's family would get together, the Jerk would somehow find a reason to be mad and pout in the corner. His silence made everyone uncomfortable, and he eventually would make Jessica leave the family function early. He would humiliate her in front of his family by making fun of Jessica and her family. If Jessica ever tried to stand up for herself or her family he would "twist her words" and Jessica would end up apologizing for making the Jerk upset. The Jerk pressured Jessica into getting engaged. Jessica hesitantly went along with the engagement and the Jerk was easily able to navigate all of her concerns. Finally, the Jerk forced himself upon her sexually. When Jessica resisted, he threatened her and began choking her. She escaped, called her mother, and her mother immediately rescued her from the relationship. Jessica's mother was unaware of the abusive and manipulative nature of her daughter's relationship. She was aware of the fact that her daughter had a problem of "always going for the wrong guy" and wanted to get her help.

This story demonstrates many classic features of an unhealthy and destructive relationship between Jessica and the Jerk. However, there are also clues as to why Jessica seems to end up in abusive relationships that are found in Jessica's childhood and in the interaction between Jessica and her family. Jessica's story will be the model from which the mysteries behind becoming a Jerk Magnet will be revealed.

Opposites Attract?

When you think of magnets that you played with as a child, you likely noticed many interesting things. You could stick magnets to each other as long as the north pole of the magnet was touching the south pole. Two north poles or two south poles would repel each other. Also, either pole could attract metal objects such as pins or paper clips. What caused these invisible forces had largely been a mystery until roughly the early 1800s. Michael Faraday and others figured out there were magnetic fields involved and because of the influence of a nearby magnet, each pin or paperclip would become temporarily magnetized. It was found that matter consisted of tiny electrically charged particles called atoms. Atoms had negative electrons floating around a positively charged nucleus. Andre-Marie Ampere found that the fundamental nature of magnetism was its association with electric currents. Magnetic force was basically a force between two currents. While the forces attracting the atoms were invisible, they were not magical as previously thought. The added effect of the tiny individually charged atomic particles created a real and powerful attractive force.

So, by calling yourself (or your loved one) a Jerk Magnet, you are likely thinking of some unseen power that attracts you magically to Jerks or attracts the Jerks to you. You probably didn't realize the metaphor of the magnet was right on the money. As the science lesson above shows, magnets exist, but they generally have no real attractive power unless they come in contact with the right material. By calling yourself a magnet, you realize that there is some tiny particle of you, some ingrained pattern of thought, feeling, or behavior that causes Jerks to be attracted to you and you to them. These ingrained currents are the structural framework of your personality and somehow create a magnetic field that powerfully attracts you to the wrong guy.

Some people don't realize their ingrained currents are contributing to the magnetic field. They see themselves as a regular north pole magnet minding their own business and then wham! They are pelted by paperclip after paperclip or worse...the dreaded South Pole Psychopath. Sooner or later these people (or their family members) will realize that their personality structure is playing a role and hopefully will have the determination and will to change the structure. In Jessica's case, her mother felt that Jessica's insecurity and desire to please others were the main causes of her difficulties. Jessica couldn't see this. Jessica was unaware of any reason why she had such a difficult time "finding the right guy." She wasn't in denial, but was simply unaware of the many thinking errors she had and saw herself as a "victim of circumstance."

✏ TAKE HOME MESSAGE #1

Before you can be demagnetized you have to understand that, like a magnet, you are filled with tiny individual experiences that work together to shape you into the person you are.

Charged Particles

The things you experience throughout your life are the particles that make you unique. These particles shape your self-esteem and view of the world. A *Charged Particle* is different. These are the memorable trail markers along your life. The things you use to define who you are.

When you tell someone your life story, these are the highlights you tell. They can be embarrassing moments, scary moments, abuses, successes, triumphs, obstacles overcome, significant relationships, heroes, tragedies, and so on. Charged Particles are the things you include in your life's story. Obviously, you can't remember every detail of your life. Usually, our minds recall our lives in moments that are edited so we can understand and make meaning out of them. The boring stuff is generally edited out, and we remember the interesting or important. Who's the editor? You are. Depending on the situation, you highlight or deemphasize certain elements of the story.

With time, meaning is attached to the story elements and retrospective explanations are given for better understanding. How many times have you heard, "Had I not had that (challenge, failure, etc.), I wouldn't be the person I am today?" This meaning and understanding usually comes long after the trial or experience happens. At the time the experience is happening, it is just that—what's happening now. So your remembering and making meaning out of the experience is what makes the experience a Charged Particle rather than just your regular particle. It means something to you.

Whether you understand it or not, the element you chose not to edit out was significant. It is a symbol of something you want to believe about yourself. When you tell someone your life story, whether you realize it or not, you are *creating* the story. You're not just listing off dates and facts. You pick out the Charged Particles.

For example, I find that the only way I remember things from my childhood is through pictures that were taken at the time. My memory of childhood works like a scrapbook. 1st birthday, 1st pet dog, etc. These images are saved in our memories with associated smells, sounds, and feelings. What is so important about the memory I have of crashing my cousin Johnny's ten-speed bike when I was eight? I don't know. I tell the story whenever someone asks me about the scar on my left pinky finger. It seems there's a story behind every scar. Emotional wounds also leave scars that begin to have meaning and significance as time goes on. Some scars have faded and are no longer visible, but we still can recall the story of the scar. We try to make meaning out of the collections of Charged Particles, and seldom do we stop to question what it is about *this* story that makes it into the life story. Also, the tricky thing about the life story is the Charged Particles included in the story will change over time and change depending on your audience. As you will see, it will take a while for Jessica to see how her Charged Particles combined to create a magnetic field, and for her parents to see how they were like electricity helping to charge the current. (More on this parental involvement later.)

✏️ **TAKE HOME MESSAGE #2**

CHARGED PARTICLES—*stuff that happens to you during your life that shapes your self-esteem and view of the world. The memorable trail markers along your life path. The things you use to define yourself.*

ELECTRIC CURRENTS—*ingrained pattern of thought, feeling, or behavior that causes Jerks to be attracted to you and you to them.*

MAGNETIC FIELDS—*Powerful attractive force between two people.*

CHAPTER TWO

Jerk Spectrum: Player to Meanipulator

Jerks come in many forms. There are litterers and loud cell-phone-talkers, Walmart-aisle kid-spankers and traffic cut-offers, red-light runners, bird-flippers, and movie loud-talkers … not to mention public-street-no-leash dog-walkers. They're everywhere. All of us do "jerky" things from time to time, but to be a capital "J" Jerk you generally have to establish a consistent pattern of jerkness that spills out into all aspects of your life. I'm going to focus on a special breed of Jerk. The relationship Jerk: mild, moderate, and severe. Let's discuss the first two forms, mild and moderate. I call them the Player and the Mean Manipulator or *Mean*ipulator for short.

The Player

Players are annoying. They usually think they are better looking than they actually are. As a matter of fact, they think they are better at everything than they actually are and tend to avoid reality checks in general. The interesting phenomenon of the player is the art of the exaggeration— the disparity between what happened and what the player would like to happen. To the player, relationships are a game, and you are a piece to be played. Players are able to convince you of their specialness. This is usually done by comparing themselves to you and trying to make you feel ordinary. They are able to make you feel like you are lucky to be with them. They are one-uppers. They are braggers. Some fancy themselves as good dancers and like to check out their dance moves in the mirror at clubs. They wouldn't think twice about showing compromising pictures of you to their friends. The word egomaniac comes to mind. Because of the Players' distorted sense of reality, they sincerely believe they can get a better relationship at any time. Like most Jerks, they are smooth talkers and wonderful flat-terers; they are able to get themselves out of trouble easily.

Okay, now it's time for your first test: Try to identify if you are in a relationship with a player.

JERK TEST #1
(Please check boxes that apply.)

☐ While on a date, he will frequently comment on other women: "Wow, she's hot."

☐ He may flirt with other women while out with you.

☐ Makes you swear not to tell anyone you are a couple.

☐ Occasionally he will forget your name, your phone number, or call you the wrong name.

☐ He will introduce you as his "friend."

☐ When he comes to pick you up for a date, he will honk the horn in front of your house.

☐ When he takes you on an expensive date, he expects you to sleep with him.

☐ He will frequently blow off your plans for his friends or work.

☐ He will sometimes conveniently "forget" his wallet on dates when the check arrives.

☐ He may act differently with you depending on the social situation.

☐ He is mildly controlling. For example, he may "suggest" you wear a certain outfit and want you to behave in a certain way.

☐ He will hold your hand until he sees a good-looking girl and then he will suddenly let go.

If more than one of these items applies to your relationship, be careful. You may be dating a Player. Players can be very charming, and are able to make you think they are sincere. Players generally avoid long-term relationships because they are constantly on the prowl. Players will frequently brag about their escapades to their friends (with the usual exaggeration of detail). A major score for Players is dating two women at the same time, or better yet, having sex with two different women in the same night.

Fortunately, after brief encounters with Players, they are easy to identify. They usually move on to perceived greener pastures swiftly. Unfortunately, the rush of the initial encounter with Players is intoxicating. They can make you feel special, but soon they begin to undermine your confidence and leave you feeling insecure and full of self-doubt. Another alluring aspect of Players is the desire to "tame the beast." You may feel that you are the woman who can turn him from his Player ways. He will love you so much he will stop playing and settle down. This has been known to happen, but it is a rarity. Players are notorious for coming back. You can't get rid of these guys. After several weeks or months, you may get a late-night call, "Hey Baby, why don't you come over and watch a movie?" Don't be fooled. Don't let him put you on his late-night speed dial.

The magnetic field surrounding the Player "paper-clip" is fairly weak. This is why he is categorized as mild on the Jerk Spectrum. Yeah, he is a Jerk, but he moves so quickly you don't have much to bond to. However, the attractive forces can be strong at first, and it might be difficult to resist repeated encounters. If you do become involved in a longer-term relationship with a Player, beware. They can sometimes go from Player to *Mean*ipulator.

The *Mean*ipulator

*Mean*ipulators are control freaks. Their goal is to have complete power over you and the relationship. *Mean*ipulators are sneaky and subtle in the way they gradually take control of your time, friends, and daily activities. Beware of this kind of guy, because he is very likely to emotionally, verbally, physically, or sexually abuse you. You may have

been flattered at first by his devotion and concern for you.
After a while, however, you may feel suffocated by his need
to constantly be with you and know what you are doing at
all times. Here are some things *Mean*ipulators do:

JERK TEST #2
(Please check boxes that apply.)

☐ *Shows up unexpectedly, doesn't pay attention to you, always keeps track of where you are, doesn't believe you, and always checks your story.*

☐ *Tries to control different aspects of your life: how you dress, who you hang out with, what you say.*

☐ *Constantly becomes jealous or angry when you want to spend time with family or friends.*

☐ *Demands to know where you are at all times.*

☐ *Says he's always right.*

☐ *Convinces you that you are worthless, unworthy of him, unattractive, dumb, or immature.*

☐ *Frequently humiliates you or belittles you.*

☐ *Twists the truth to make you feel you are to blame for his actions.*

☐ *Tries to persuade you that no one would ever find you attractive, that you are somehow damaged.*

As your relationship with a *Mean*ipulator progresses, he may try to control you with statements like, "If you really loved me you would ..." The scary thing about these people is their controlling tactics can easily turn to emotional and physical abuse. In his attempt to control you, he may yell at you and call you names. If he ever has harmed you or threatened to harm you in any way, this is relationship abuse. It is hard to define relationship abuse, and usually a one-time incident does not constitute abuse. You are in an abusive relationship if there is a repeated pattern of negative and destructive behaviors that escalate over time. Jerk Test #2 and Abuse Test (next page) are extremely important. If you check any of the boxes below, this is not normal. Stop reading. Put down the book and call the National Domestic Violence Hotline 1-800-799-SAFE (7233). This service is available to callers 24 hours a day, 365 days a year. When you call, trained counselors will provide assistance and information about legal advice, counseling, health care centers, and shelters. Please go to the Resources section at the end of this book for more details.

ABUSE TEST
(Please check boxes that apply.)

- ☐ Slapping
- ☐ Pushing
- ☐ Hurting or killing pets
- ☐ Shaking
- ☐ Kicking
- ☐ Smacking
- ☐ Holding you down

- ☐ Biting
- ☐ Cutting
- ☐ Punching
- ☐ Choking
- ☐ Destroying property
- ☐ Physical intimidation
- ☐ Rape or other sexual abuse

A *Mean*ipulator who becomes an abuser may put you down but tell you he still loves you. He may have you believing it is your fault you are being abused. "I'm sorry but if you hadn't …blah, blah, blah, then I wouldn't have had to blah, blah." He may coerce or threaten to harm you if you leave the relationship. This is not normal. You may think this is just a normal part of a relationship and it will be worked out somehow. No. This is abuse and you are in a relationship with a controlling *Mean*ipulator. How does this happen?

They are sneaky about it. If the *Mean*ipulator acted like this on day one, hopefully you would run away. They start by putting on a good show for you, and then they do a bait-and-switch or what I call the 180.

The 180

In Jessica's case, her boyfriend/fiancé wasn't initially a jerk. He was a kind and handsome guy who played on the rugby team of the local college. They met when a roommate introduced them after a rugby game and Jessica was immediately attracted to his charm and "take charge" quality. He was a natural leader of his small group of friends, and this leadership quality also was attractive. Jessica says that he changed when she agreed to marry him. "It was like he became a different person," she recalls. The most striking element of his 180 was his sense of entitlement. He suddenly began to treat Jessica as his property. He began to act as if he had a right to her body. All of a sudden there was this expectation that wasn't there before. He expected her to do what he said. He also began to be closed off to her. He would say, "I don't have to tell you what I'm feeling or thinking." Unfortunately for Jessica, she was already committed to him and thought that she must have done something wrong for him to change so much. She would think to herself, "I know this guy, he's not like this. I must be causing this." Jessica began to feel responsible for her significant other's behavior. Whenever they would get into an argument, she would be the one to "give in." She had difficulty sticking up for herself, and would rather be unhappy than have the Jerk angry with her. Jessica was so caught up in the relationship, she easily would excuse his behavior. "He's really stressed out with school," or "He's been working so hard lately." Although initially it felt like a 180-degree change, Jessica is now able to see that there were many warning signs that her boyfriend was indeed a *Mean*ipulator all along.

The good news is after reading this book, you will be better able to spot the warning signs of *Mean*ipulators and show them the door before they can do a 180 on you.

The Drama and the Passion

In addition to being blinded by a Jerk's true character, another reason you may find yourself in a relationship with a *Mean*ipulator, or even a *Mean*ipulator turned abuser, is the drama and the passion. People who have not been in a relationship with a *Mean*ipulator don't understand how dramatic it can be. The romance is rocky. There are many ups and downs with long hours invested in discussion. There is an element of desperation in trying to keep the relationship alive. Everything in the relationship with a *Mean*ipulator is exaggerated. Jessica tried many times to "cool down" the relationship with her Jerk early on. He would become irate and make public scenes. He had no shame in crying or threatening to harm himself unless she took him back.

*Mean*ipulators are skilled at upping the ante. They are able to focus in on your weaknesses and find the right button to push to get results. For Jessica, her guilt feelings were so strong, all the Jerk had to do was threaten suicide and she would stop all talk of breaking off the engagement. If you ever hear the words, "If you leave me, I don't know what I would do," or "It will be your fault if something bad happens," this is drama and you are being manipulated. Like many, Jessica misinterpreted the exaggerated highs and lows in her relationship as a strong bond. The Jerk made her believe the many battles they had endured were a sign that they were "supposed" to be together. The drama and the passion of a relationship like this can be very misleading and give you a false sense of normalcy. This is not normal. Don't believe that if a relationship does not have the drama and desperation it is not as strong. Also, don't buy into the notion that because you have invested so much time, energy, tears, and effort into the relationship that the relationship should be continued because of the equity you have built up. The relationship you've been investing in has a crack in the foundation and you need to cut your losses and move on.

The magnetic field surrounding the *Mean*ipulator can be strong, and this is why he is categorized as moderate on the Jerk Spectrum. While there are a lot of Players out there, the majority of you who call yourself (or loved one) a Jerk Magnet are dealing with the *Mean*ipulator, and this is why you should pay special attention to their patterns of behavior. It will also be important for you to think openly and honestly about your ingrained patterns of thought and behavior. The buttons the *Mean*ipulator pushes are based on your own Charged Particles. At first, Jessica was unable to recognize how her self-image and personality structure were contributing to the magnetic field. Shortly, I will discuss Jessica's childhood and teenage years, and it will become clear how the Electric Current (also known as her ingrained pattern of thinking) greatly contributed to her becoming a Jerk Magnet. But first, you must know about the most dangerous and sinister of the Jerks. The top of the Jerk food chain … the South Pole Psychopath.

✎ TAKE HOME MESSAGE #3

Players—mild on the Jerk Spectrum. Beware: they can be charmers. They will use you and undermine your confidence.

Meanipulators—moderate on the Jerk Spectrum. They are controllers and can easily be abusers. Beware of the exaggerated, dramatic, rocky relationship with this entitled Jerk.

An abusive relationship is not normal. If you checked any boxes on the Abuse Test you shouldn't be reading this unless you have called the National Domestic Violence Hotline 1-800-799-SAFE (7233). I mean it. Stop. Put this book down. Call for help.

CHAPTER THREE

The South Pole Psychopath

"He's just plain psycho," is a common statement used when dealing with Jerks. You may have used it yourself. It is a common slang term to describe someone whose behavior doesn't make sense to us. The media may incorrectly use it to describe someone with mental illness. You may remember the Alfred Hitchcock thriller, *Psycho* where the Norman Bates character dresses up like his mother and kills people. The word "psycho" can conjure up many images of the madman lurking in the bushes, serial killers, and so on. Psycho is short for Psychopath or Psychopathy—which can be a confusing terms. Literally, it means "mind disease" from *psyche* and *pathos*. The dictionary will define it as a mentally ill or deranged person, especially someone with Antisocial Personality Disorder. So what is a psychopath? How is a psychopath different from a sociopath? And what is Antisocial Personality Disorder? Answer—they are all different names for the same kind of person. The difference depends on what context you're talking about and who you're talking to. The term reflects the user's perspective on what causes the condition. Some sociologists and criminologists believe the condition is shaped entirely by social forces and early life experience. They prefer the term sociopath. Others who feel that genetic, biological, and psychological factors contribute to the condition prefer the term psychopath. The technical term that is accepted by most clinicians and researchers is Antisocial Personality Disorder. This last term is also confusing because most people think that the term antisocial means you're against socializing. People mistakenly think antisocial means you'd prefer to stay home and play video games or chat online rather that go to a party or the mall. Antisocial Personality Disorder is defined by the

American Psychiatric Association's DSM-V ("Diagnostic Bible") by the following criteria:

> A pattern of disregard for others and violation of the rights of others since the age of 15. Patients must be at least 18 years old for this diagnosis and three or more of the following must be present:
>
> - Failure to conform to social norms by committing unlawful acts
> - Deceitfulness/repeated lying/manipulating others for personal gain
> - Impulsive/failure to plan ahead
> - Irritability and aggressiveness/repeated fights or assaults
> - Recklessness and disregard for safety of self and others
> - Irresponsibility/failure to sustain work or honor financial obligations
> - Lack of remorse for actions.[1]

A person with Antisocial Personality Disorder or what I call a South Pole Psychopath is the most severe form of Jerk. He is in a class by himself. While Jerks and *Mean*ipulators are bad, they are nothing compared to the attractive force and ability of the psychopath. In my experience

---

1 American Psychiatric Association (2013). *Diagnostic and Statistical Manual: Mental Disorders* (rev. 5th ed.) Washington, D.C.: Author.

with these kinds of people, I find they tend to view people as objects to be manipulated. They don't care about the feelings and rights of others. They are morally bankrupt and lack a sense of remorse. The tricky part is they can be very charming and engaging on the outside, but underneath is a person who lives in a world of lies, lies to cover other lies, illegal activity, promiscuity, and darkness. It is estimated by the National Institute of Mental Health that approximately 3 men out of 100 will meet criteria for the diagnosis. That means 2 to 3 million in North America alone. You can imagine a high percentage of these people would be caught by police and it's true that approximately 75% of the prison population carry the diagnosis. Early predictors of future antisocials include multiple delinquent acts before the age of 10 and a diagnosis of Conduct Disorder ("Antisocial Junior") before the age of 15. Conduct Disorder basically is a pattern of behavior that involves the violation of social norms, rules, and the basic rights of others with at least three of the following:

- Aggression toward people and animals

- Destruction of property

- Deceitfulness

- Serious violations of rules

Another term that gets confused in the mix is *psychotic* or *psychosis*. This term is used to describe a mental or behavioral disorder that causes severe distortion or disorganization of a person's mental capacity. A person with psychosis cannot recognize reality and has difficulty communicating and relating with others. We all can have symptoms of psychosis from time to time. For example, after surgery, it is very common to have distortions of reality while one is in the hospital and on high doses of pain medication. A person may confuse the IV pole and IV tubing for a tree and a snake. This illusion or misperception of reality is a common form of psychosis. Brain tumors, strokes, and seizures can also cause a person to become psychotic. Mental illnesses such as schizophrenia, bipolar disorder, and even major depression can have elements of psychosis. You probably have heard the term insanity, or that someone was not guilty by reason of insanity. This is now an outmoded term, but it is still used in legal circles to signify that a person is so impaired by their mental illness they don't have the capacity to make decisions and should not be held legally responsible for their actions. For example, if someone is truly psychotic, they might believe that the postal worker is not really a postal worker, but might see a hallucination of a grizzly bear instead. They may sincerely believe they are deep in the woods rather than in their own home. If a psychotic person mistakenly shoots and injures the postal worker while thinking they are protecting themselves from a grizzly, they legitimately were "not in their right mind" at the time. They would not be able to understand the significance of the situation and a judge would likely find them not guilty by reason of insanity.

For the most part, a psychopath is not psychotic and not insane. They are able to realize exactly what they are doing and know they are breaking the rules. They just don't care. They can repeatedly be caught and even sent to prison, but that doesn't stop them from breaking the rules. This is the problem with the psychopath. The fear of punishment is not strong enough to stop them from doing what they want to do. It is considered a mental illness, but since the person with this personality style has insight and control over his behavior, he is considered competent and thus, accountable for his behavior. Psychopaths are good at convincing a judge that they have another mental illness, such as bipolar disorder, and are in need of psychiatric hospitalization. They are able to manipulate the system to avoid jail time. For a short time, they are able to control their behavior while in the mental hospital to get on the good side of the doctor and staff. They then begin to demand to leave because they are either cured of their mental illness or they become such difficult patients they are discharged. A person with psychosis does not have the insight to pull off such schemes.

In the classic book, *The Mask of Sanity,* Dr. Hervey Cleckley explains the meaning of the psychopath's behavior:

> It is impossible for him to take even a slight
> interest in the tragedy or joy or the striving of

humanity as presented in serious literature or art. He is also indifferent to all these matters in life itself. Beauty and ugliness, except in a very superficial sense, goodness, evil, love, horror, and humor have no actual meaning, no power to move him. He is, furthermore, lacking in the ability to see that others are moved. It is as though he were color-blind, despite his sharp intelligence, to this aspect of human existence. It cannot be explained to him because there is nothing in his orbit of awareness that can bridge the gap with comparison. He can repeat the words and say glibly that he understands, and there is no way for him to realize that he does not understand.[2]

It is very difficult to understand what Dr. Cleckley tries to convey unless you've had contact with a person like this. Cleckley's work also provides a glimpse into the behavior of a female psychopath, which illustrates a good point...males don't have the market cornered when it comes to being a Jerk. There are female Jerks out there, which will briefly be discussed in Chapter 6.

To better illustrate a psychopath in the wild, here's an example of the way a psychopath lies and manipulates:

---

2 Cleckly, Hervey. *The Mask of Sanity.* St. Louis, MO: Mosby. 1976, 90.

Anna met Dillon in the summer of 2004 while she was working at a community center. Dillon began meeting her for her lunch breaks, for her bus rides home; every time she walked out of the building, Dillon was there waiting. He told her very little about himself. Sometimes he carried large amounts of money, other times he was broke. He talked constantly, describing all his ideas, schemes, and plans, which never amounted to anything. Whenever she asked him about some plan he'd concocted in the past, he seemed annoyed. "Oh that, I'm way past that, I'm doing something way better now."

One day, while they were having coffee at Starbucks, police arrived and he was arrested and booked into jail. The next day Anna went to visit him. The police said he'd spent the night at a friend's house and the next day had stolen and sold the man's computer equipment. It turned out that Dillon was wanted by the police for many other charges and he went to prison.

He wrote to Anna from prison at least once every day, sometimes as many as five times a day. He wrote of his talents, his dreams, his plans. If only Dillon could find the right situation, the right plan, he'd be on top of the world, he'd be able to do "anything." Because of his "devotion" to her, she wasn't even fazed by his repeated requests for her to send money.

In 13 months, Dillon was out. He went directly to Anna's house and tried propositioning her. When that didn't work, he tried propositioning her roommates. He was able to get the women to allow him to move in with them. This guy was good.

It was soon clear that he had no intention of leaving and no intention of finding a job. Still, Anna kept trying to find work for him. The first interview he had was successful, but his first day on the job he took the company van on a joy ride and then disappeared for five days. Then a friend called to tell Anna that Dillon was dealing drugs. When she confronted him, he denied everything. And she believed him.

She decided to break it off with Dillon. He grabbed her arm, pushed her to the ground, put a knee to her back and said, "You'll never get away from me; I'll always be with you baby." Within days, she moved to another apartment—and Dillon began to stalk her. Messages reached her—he'd kill himself if she didn't see him, he'd never let up until she did. But then the messages changed. Dillon wasn't going to kill himself; he was going to kill Anna. Soon afterward, he found her, broke down the door to her apartment, and pushed her down. Luckily, her new roommate came home early and stopped him. At the sight of her roommate,

Dillon calmed down instantly. He acted as if everything was fine and left the apartment.

He never returned. For years afterward, Anna got reports that Dillon had been arrested, mostly for fraud, twice for assault, and some kind of scam with a helicopter flight school that didn't exist. The last she heard, he was back in prison. Often she wondered how she could have trusted him so completely from the beginning.

It was not entirely Anna's fault that she was attracted to Dillon. He was charming and caring at first. He undoubtedly did a 180-degree change at some point during their relationship, but at that point Anna was already invested in him. She was mesmerized by his "big plans." Dillon was able to smooth talk his way out of any situation. You probably were able to see how Dillon progressed in his manipulation to the point of violence. He verbally threatened her by making statements like, "I'll never let you go." When he found his threats no longer worked, he resorted to violence. This verbal intimidation is a classic tactic used by *Mean*ipulators and South Pole Psychopaths. The South Pole Psychopath takes it to the next level. He's a professional manipulator. As the manipulation escalates to violence, some psychopaths don't have far to go until murder becomes a logical option. In the mind of a psychopath, you are an object to be manipulated, a tool, a product. If killing you works to their advantage, some psychopaths will do it without a second thought. To a South Pole Psychopath, murder can be an option to escape the web of lies they have created.

In Emmanuel Carrere's book, *The Adversary: A True Story of Monstrous Deception,* the story is told of Jean-Claude Romand who deceived his family and friends by posing as a physician for the World Health Organization. He began his medical studies in France, but failed out of medical school during his second year. He somehow was able to convince his wife, parents, and best friend that he was still in medical school and for the next 13 years posed as a well-respected physician. He would leave for work every day and spend his day reading in the library or walking in the county side. He would travel to the World Health Organization Headquarters and collect pamphlets and discarded documents to display in his car or on the desk at home. He would go on fake business trips and stay for several days at a time at the airport hotel. He was able to survive by stealing money from his parents' retirement or by selling phony "new research medication" to neighbors and relatives with the promise that it would cure their cancer. His deception came to an end when he began a relationship with another woman and took her money to "invest" in supposed high yield investments. When his mistress discovered his scam, and his lifetime of lies was on the verge being exposed, Carrere chillingly describes how his psychopathic reasoning concluded that it would be better for his wife, two small children, and elderly parents to die rather than be shamed by his false life. On January 9, 1993, he brutally shot his two children, his wife, and parents and then made a half-hearted attempt to commit suicide by consuming a low dose of an expired sedative and setting his house on fire. He was rescued by firefighters and concocted a new story that intruders killed his family. During the investigation, his deception was revealed and he was sent to prison, but only given 25 years to life. He was up for parole in 2015.[3]

Another example of a web of lies that leads to murder is the story of Mark Hacking. On July 19, 2004, Mark Hacking faced the news cameras and made an emotional plea for help in finding his missing wife Lori. He said she went running earlier that morning and he became nervous when he found out she hadn't reported to work. Her car was found abandoned at a nearby park. The next day, hundreds of missing person signs were seen in the couple's hometown of Salt Lake City, and over a thousand volunteers gathered to help in the search. The memory of Elizabeth Smart's abduction was still fresh in the minds of the people of Salt Lake, and they were more than willing to help to ensure Lori's safety and the safety of the community.

Mark and Lori had been married for ten years and by all accounts had a wonderful marriage. Mark was supposedly an Honors graduate of the University of Utah and had

---

3 Carrere, Emmanuel. *The Adversary: A True Story of Monstrous Deception.* Picador, New York 2000.

been accepted to medical school in North Carolina. The couple was preparing to move, and Lori was preparing to quit her job. People who knew Mark commented that he was always studying medical books. Co-workers reported that even on his breaks he would find a quiet room to study practice MCAT (Medical College Admission Test) questions. Mark's father and brother were doctors, and Mark was excited to be joining such a noble profession. Except for the fact that he wasn't going to medical school and he hadn't even finished college.

Early on, police classified Mark as a "person of interest" in the case. They thought it was peculiar that the driver's seat of Lori's abandoned car was set for someone over 6 feet tall and Lori was only 5' 4". A search of the apartment revealed a new queen size mattress, a bloody knife in a drawer, and Lori's car keys. Also, it was discovered that at the time Mark said he was searching for Lori, credit card records revealed he was actually buying a new mattress.

Similar to Jean-Claude Romand in *The Adversary,* Mark had spent years weaving the tapestry of his false life.

It began to unravel when Lori called the University of North Carolina to inquire about financial issues relating to medical school. She was told that they had no record of Mark Hacking being enrolled. When Lori confronted Mark, he coolly said that there must be some kind of computer error. Mark was unwavering in his dedication to his false life, and like a good South Pole Psychopath was able to lie his way out of trouble. However, Mark's lie quickly came apart, and on the evening of July 18th he made a choice to shoot Lori. Of course, if he could get rid of Lori he could say he was too distraught to focus on medical school. Some of you may be thinking, "Just come clean" or "He should've just walked away." That's because you don't have Antisocial Personality Disorder. For Mark, this was the only way out. It was the logical choice. He was able to dispassionately shoot his pregnant wife of ten years, put her in a garbage bag, and throw her body in a dumpster. He was able to create the story of her disappearance and fabricate tears for the camera. He did not feel emotion, but he knew what someone in distress was supposed to feel and was able to go through the motions.

While South Pole Psychopaths can resort to violence and even murder, it is important to remember that most manage to take advantage of people without resorting to murder. It's more likely we would lose our life's savings to or vote for a political psychopath than be murdered by one.

You've probably noticed that the South Pole Psychopath has many elements of the Player and the Meanipulator. He is every bit as sneaky and subtle and he is the smoothest of the smooth talkers. He also wants to have complete power over you and the relationship. In addition to the things that Players and Meanipulators do, the following is a list of things that set South Pole Psychopaths apart from regular Jerks:

- Extremely egocentric with impossibly big plans.
- They have little understanding of the qualifications for their "big plan" and no good idea of how to achieve their goal.
- Not embarrassed by revealing past personal, legal, or financial problems.
- Unable to tolerate differing opinions.
- A surprising lack of concern for the pain of others.
- Are never really sorry for the destruction or pain they have caused.

- Almost magical ability to rationalize or minimize their behavior.
- Will sometimes use as excuses for their behavior: memory loss, previous head injury, amnesia, blackouts, drug use, multiple personality, alter ego, or temporary insanity.
- Do not have deep connections with people.
- View people (including family members) as objects or possessions equal to an Ipod, car, or computer.
- Naturally gifted at lying and are even proud of it.
- When caught in a lie they never get shaken or embarrassed.
- When caught in a lie they easily reconstruct the facts to align with their version of the "truth."
- Have very shallow emotions and are good at "acting" like they have true feeling.
- Will tell stories that always put themselves in a good light.
- Will seem too good to be true.
- Tend to be superficial.

The magnetic field surrounding the South Pole Psychopath can be very strong, which is why he is categorized as severe on the Jerk Spectrum. He is able to use all the tools in the Jerk Toolbox. He has mastered the Player and is the ultimate *Mean*ipulator. He will rob you, use you, lie to you, and throw you away. He is able to sense your weakness and will keep coming back to you. So, how do you repel this attractive force? Here are some suggestions.

Realize what you've got

It is important to realize that you're dealing with a person who may have a personality disorder. They can be any gender, young or old, rich or poor. It is hard to admit that your boyfriend, husband, son, or other family member may indeed be a psychopath. Use this chapter as a guide, and if you have more concerns, contact a mental health professional.

Don't look them in the eye

This may sound funny, but psychopaths are known for their blank emotionless stare. It can be very unnerving. Predators are also known for their "predatory stare" when they are sizing up their prey for the kill. This is one reason why it is recommended that you don't make eye contact with wild or stray animals. They are wired to have a fight or flight response to another animal that is staring at them. There are some butterflies that have developed big spots on their wings that look like staring eyes to ward off birds that may want to eat them. Some professionals feel that psychopaths use this intense stare to control and manipulate you. The stare can be hypnotic; look away.

Beware of the flash

Think of the con-man or magician. They use slight of hand and distraction to divert your attention to what is really going on. In this same way, the psychopath will use his good looks, sexy smile, body language, and fast talk to mesmerize and seduce you. If you find yourself responding to one of these elements of a person's personality in an overwhelming way, stop. Think. Listen to what they are actually saying. Don't be fooled by smoke and mirrors.

Get the history

When you first meet someone, it is common to talk about your past. Many times you try to make connections to find things you may have in common with your new romantic interest. Ask him about his friends, where he works, his family, where he lives. This doesn't have to be on the first date or while you're sitting at the bar, but ask sometime. Beware of the hazy, vague, and inconsistent past history. If he becomes uncomfortable with you asking about his past and seems suspicious or guarded, he may be hiding something.

Believe it, people lie

Most people lie a little. We know we shouldn't. It's almost human nature to embellish stories from our past to present ourselves in a better light. As a kid, I used to make up stories that pirates buried their treasure at Lorenzi Park. I had my brother and other neighborhood kids believing that the pirates somehow trekked some 600 miles from the nearest ocean to the desert of Las Vegas to bury their treasure. I guess I liked the attention. Oh yeah, and kids are dumb… myself included.

Sometimes we tell lies to protect others when we feel the truth may be harmful or distressing to them. When I was in medical school, a classmate of mine failed Anatomy. It was the school policy that you could retake the class the next year and finish school in five years rather than the customary four. Unfortunately, he failed the class again and was dismissed from the school. Unknown to me, he didn't tell his wife that he failed out of medical school and continued to leave in the morning as usual and return in the evening with talk of tests, labs, and so on. I remember seeing him several months later with his wife in the grocery store. I knew he was dismissed from school and said, "Hey man, what you been up to now that you have some free time?" I'll never forget his large-eyed look as he held his finger to his lips. "Shhhh. My wife doesn't know I'm not in school." Later, I found out that he and his wife were trying to get pregnant and he didn't want his wife upset by knowing he was kicked out of medical school. I'm not saying this guy was a psychopath, but you can see how trying to protect someone from the truth by lying only will lead to more problems. And come to think of it, maybe he was a psychopath.

Lying is lying whatever the intent or desire. How is the psychopath different? It is a matter of degree. We usually know where the truth stops and the lie begins. Psychopaths don't. A psychopath lies so much he believes his lies are reality. He will tell his story so often it will become true to him. This is how they are able to beat lie detector tests. You know, it's not a lie if you believe it's true. Again, if you confront a suspected psychopath with the truth, be aware of how they rework the story to conform to their lie. If you press them, they will turn the focus of their wrath towards you. They will make you feel you are the one with the problem and are being too hard on them. If you find that you are always apologizing after these encounters, you may be a north pole magnet in the midst of the magnetic influence of a South Pole Psychopath. Beware of the stare. Beware of the flash. Run.

CHAPTER FOUR

The Mysteries of Magnetism

Did Jessica have bad luck? Was she just a terrible judge of character? Maybe she didn't learn from her mistakes. Jessica was going through life like many people do. She had dreams and goals and was making an effort to navigate the dating scene to find "Mr. Right." From her standpoint, she went from relationship to relationship in a passive, non-threatening, non-aggressive way, and somehow kept finding "Mr. Wrong." Her mother was convinced that Jessica's insecurity was the core issue. "She just doesn't have confidence in herself" her mother would say. It's hard to fathom that Jessica would be lacking in self-confidence. She was attractive and stylish. She obviously would not have any trouble getting dates. So why did she end up with a Jerk every time? While her mother was right, insecurity was a core issue, there was much more to it. A look into the Charged Particles of her early childhood and adolescence will help uncover the mystery of her magnetism.

Early Childhood

Jessica was the oldest of four children (two sisters, one brother). Her parents were married throughout her life and she described their relationship as "ideal." There were arguments in the home, but generally her parents kept open communication and discussed issues until they could be resolved. Jessica's father was a large, dominant figure who worked as a land developer. He did not have a college education and took pride in his ability to "have money" without going to college. Jessica described her father as the "perfect dad." She admired how he was a leader in the home and in the community. He was a "take charge" kind of guy and knew how to get things done. Jessica's mother was a very involved perfectionist with "high standards." If there were any problems in the family, Jessica's mother made sure that it was kept within the family. It was extremely important to deal with issues in the home and not let others know of any difficulty. Her mother had a way of making her children feel guilty if they didn't perform at a very high level. Jessica became desperate for her mother's approval during these years, and found that is was easier to agree with others than to stand up for her own thoughts and feelings.

When Jessica began school, it was discovered that she had a mild learning disability and had to attend resource classes throughout her elementary school years. In keeping with the family theme of dealing with problems within the family, Jessica's mother kept the learning disability a secret from everyone, including Jessica. Jessica did not understand at first why she had to be in the special classes and said that she felt hurt that her mother did not tell her the purpose of the classes. It didn't take long for Jessica to figure out she was intellectually "different" and she was teased "mercilessly" by her classmates. Jessica felt inferior to the other children. She desperately wanted to have friends, but felt they would not accept her. She began to let the children "boss" her around. They would take her toys or "borrow" her clothes with friendship as the reward for her cooperation. Jessica did not want trouble with these kids and said she "went along with it so they would like me." She hated conflict and tried her best to avoid all conflict with friends and family. Because of her learning difficulties, Jessica began to see herself as "defective." She felt she was lucky if anybody liked her at all. After a while, Jessica found she needed her friends and family to make decisions for her. She began to lose confidence in her ability to think and make decisions for herself.

So what do these things have to do with Jessica becoming a Jerk Magnet? Well, several themes emerged from Jessica's early childhood that would play a big part in the creation of her magnetism.

- She saw herself as defective and lost confidence in her ability to make decisions.
- She learned early in life to keep thoughts, emotions, and feelings inside, especially if there was a problem.
- She desperately sought the approval of others.

- She developed a pattern of conflict avoidance.
- She developed an inability to stand up for herself.
- The male figure of the family should be a "take charge" kind of guy.

These themes in Jessica's life had been there since she was very young, and she didn't even know it. From her earliest years, these themes began to shape her personality and her view of herself. After reading the description of Jessica's early home life, you probably can understand how this happened; she learned these things from her parents and home environment. But it's much more complicated than that. It's also important to talk about why this happened.

Child Development Made Easy

Okay, we are now going to talk a little bit about child development. Wait, before you run for the door, this will be child development made easy, not boring psychological mumbo jumbo. Relax.

There are many theories of how children develop and of what is "normal" and "abnormal" development. The basic idea is that from birth to the adult years there is a series of things children learn how to do and they do them in a somewhat predictable order. If you think of a child learning how to roll over, pick up a toy, sit up, pull up, and walk, you know that kids usually don't walk before they can roll over. During these early months, their brains grow and develop rapidly. They may have the strength to walk, but until their brains catch up and figure out balance, they will continue to crawl. They develop step by step. Child researchers believe that there are psychological steps that we have to go through in order to become healthy, well-adjusted adults.

One of the first psychological steps is developing basic trust with the caregiver. This tie that binds the child to caregiver is called *attachment* and it begins in the first few hours of life. Attachment can be made with more than one person and can be in varying strengths. Infants are smart and quickly learn ways to get attention—which strengthens the attachment. They cry, smile, cling, cuddle, wave, reach their arms up to you so you'll pick them up, etc. Let's face it; babies are good at getting what they want. If we are securely attached from a young age, we feel safe to explore the world around us. We develop a sense of who we are and can be independent from our caregiver. In short, we feel secure. This security helps us learn to be responsible and accountable, to share, and to cooperate with others. We learn how to deal with fear and anxiety. If attachment doesn't occur or is disrupted, we feel insecure. This insecurity can influence every aspect of our lives and greatly influence the way we attach to others in the future.

Researchers have done extensive study to help us understand how these developmental steps explain how a person moves from being dependent and clingy to being psychologically independent. People who successfully move through the steps are no longer dependent on others to guide them. They have a sense of who they are and can get close to others without fearing they will lose their identity.

Researchers believe that if you don't complete the steps successfully, you basically get stuck at that level of emotional development. In a way, you become impaired and may feel insecure and unsafe. You feel unaccepted and respond to stress, anxiety, and conflict in a way a child would. For example, when healthy, well-adjusted people get into a disagreement, they usually don't throw a tantrum to get what they want. Most likely, they attempt to communicate their wishes and their point of view. Hopefully, they will try to see things from the other person's point of view and come to a compromise. If for some reason they have not developed emotionally past say a 12 or 13 year old, they may indeed throw a fit, stomp, yell, or cry until the other person does what is wanted. They regress.

Regression is the idea that you emotionally go backwards. Even well-adjusted people who have gone through the maturation steps can regress back to younger levels during times of intense stress or depression. Why does this happen? Security. It is thought people regress back to a level where they felt secure, which can be all the way back to the thumb sucking days for some.

Like the child who has the leg strength to walk but the brain has not advanced to the point of being able to balance, sometimes our emotional development is not as developed as our physical or intellectual development. Think of the emotional development as being malnourished or even starved to the point where it becomes emaciated. Physical, verbal, emotional, and sexual abuse can be big causes of emotional emaciation. Other causes can be neglect or early childhood loss of a loved one. The list of causes can go on and on. This emotional emaciation can take on additional significance when added to our life story. Like scars that fade over time, these emotionally Charged Particles become ingrained in the way we see ourselves and the world around us. We may not even remember the emotional wound that damaged our ability to attach and destroyed our feeling of security, because the mind has a way of protecting itself from painful memories by burying them deep inside.

Now the purpose of the child-development-made-easy lecture is not for you to say, "I knew it, it's all my parents' fault," but to show that there are complex issues going on in the creation of the Charged Particles that shaped your self-esteem and your view of the world. There are attachment issues, a step-by-step emotional maturation process, regression … basically, a bunch of stuff that you may or may not have control over.

Attachment issues may factor into the formation of Jessica's themes of seeking approval and loss of ability to make decisions. Perhaps her feelings of being defective were so overwhelming she began to build her self-esteem by pleasing others (by being an obedient daughter, not causing problems in the family, etc.) in an attempt to compensate. Because she placed so much emphasis on pleasing others and making sure everyone was happy, any disappointment or unhappiness was interpreted by Jessica as, "They don't love me." This feeling of rejection caused Jessica to hate conflict and avoid it at all costs. She rarely would get in an argument with others and if she did, she would quickly back down. Not a secure way to start adolescence.

Adolescence

By the time Jessica was fifteen her self-esteem was at an all-time low. She continually sought approval from others to help her feel good about herself. This was when she met her first boyfriend, Brad. Brad was a senior at their high school and was the lead in the high school musical. Brad was talented and Jessica felt lucky to be dating him. After a while, Brad began to get annoyed with Jessica because he felt she could never make up her mind. If he asked her where she wanted to go on a date, Jessica would say, "I don't know … where ever you want." Also, Brad was into appearances and he felt that Jessica was overweight. He would make comments to her like, "Are you going to eat that?" and "You probably don't need to be eating that." So, although she was fifteen, 5'5", and weighed 100 pounds, she began restricting her diet for him. In Dr. Hilde Bruch's, The Golden Cage, the core issue behind eating disorders is discussed and it's amazing how it matches with Jessica's personality style.

> Many anorexics express themselves in similar ways…that their whole life had been an ordeal of wanting to live up to the expectations of their families, always fearing they were not good enough in comparison with others and, therefore, disappointing failures. This dramatic dissatisfaction is a core issue in anorexia nervosa.[4]

---

4 Bruch, Hilde, M.D. *The Golden Cage.* (1978) Harvard University Press.

Jessica's insecurity and low self-esteem, coupled with her desire to please Brad caused her to become dangerously underweight. She wanted to be perfect for Brad, which meant she would be whatever he wanted. Brad broke up with her after about four months. Jessica was devastated and was sure it was because she had done something wrong.

While Brad was likely a Player, her next boyfriend, Max, was a downright *Mean*ipulator. Max started out charming and smooth. He was an athlete and liked to party. Again, Jessica was flattered that he liked her and did her best to make the relationship work. After a while, though, Max began to make her feel "worthless." He was critical of her appearance and clothing style. He would tell her what to wear and who she could hang out with. After about six months of dating, Max left to join the Marines. His final words to her were, "You better not date anyone while I'm gone, and besides, nobody would want you anyway." Jessica believed him.

The next several years were punctuated by Rob, Sebastian, and Steven all with similar stories of manipulation. It took several years for Jessica to stop restricting her diet. She reported that she liked the control she felt by restricting her intake and it helped her to cope with her insecurity.

Jessica eventually graduated high school and her parents encouraged her to attend the local community college. Because of her learning disability, college was difficult. She was able to finish an Associates Degree and had a desire to become a high school teacher. However, she became frustrated and tired with college. At her parent's suggestion, she enrolled in cosmetology school. You can see that her feeling of security in her ability to make decisions is not very strong. She clung to her parents and did not know how to be psychologically independent. Her inability to make decisions, desire to please her parents, and discomfort with conflict, made her feel trapped. She was a ship without a rudder. She didn't know what she thought or needed, and believed others knew what was best for her. She had developed a dependent personality style.

A personality is uh, you know...

So what is a personality? Good question. I talked briefly about the Antisocial Personality Disorder in Chapter 3, but never really talked about a personality. We probably ought to talk about what a personality is in order to understand how it can be disordered.

In simple terms, the ingrained pattern of feelings, behavior, thought, and the way you adapt to the world is your personality. This personality makes you a unique individual and is as a result of genetic, biological, social, cultural, and environmental factors. Family influence has a lot to do with the development of your personality. Sometimes we get along better with our parents, brother, or sister because our personalities are similar. Also, we butt heads with certain family members because our personalities are so different. Personalities are as unique and varied as the billions of humans on the planet. There are some things that a good number of people do that allow them to be put in a personality category. For example, there are enough people out there who lie, manipulate, break the law, fail to plan ahead, and lack empathy or remorse that someone said, "Hey, these people all act the same and their pattern is predictable ... let's put them in a category." Hence, we have the South Pole Psychopath. The difficulty is many people don't just fit into one category. You might have a little of this style, or a little of that. Although it can be fun to get a DSM V and diagnose your friends and loved ones, only a trained professional should use the DSM V to diagnose mental conditions. That being said, it is still important to know about the various personality styles and have an understanding of when a personality style can become a disorder.

The DSM V gives general criteria for a personality disorder:

An enduring pattern of inner experience and behavior that deviates markedly from the expectations of the individual's culture. This pattern is manifested in two (or more) of the following:

1. Cognition (ways of perceiving and interpreting self, other people, and events)
2. Affectivity (the range, intensity, liability, and appropriateness of emotional response)

3. Interpersonal functioning
4. Impulse control

The enduring pattern is inflexible and pervasive across a broad range of personal and social situations.

The enduring pattern leads to clinically significant distress or impairment in social, occupational, or other important areas of functioning.

The pattern is stable and of long duration, and its onset can be traced back at least to adolescence or early childhood.

The enduring pattern is not better accounted for as a manifestation or consequence of another mental disorder.

The enduring pattern is not due to the direct physiological effects of a substance (a drug of abuse, a medication) or a general medical condition (head trauma). [5]

So you'll notice a key phrase that is repeated is an "enduring pattern." The pattern of behavior has been there for a long time and causes trouble in a person's job, social life,

---

5 American Psychiatric Association (2013). *Diagnostic and Statistical Manual: Mental Disorders* (rev. 5th ed.) Washington, D.C.: Author.

personal, and family relationships. It also should be noted that this pattern of behavior is not caused by medication, drugs, a medical condition, or another mental disorder. The DSM V categorizes 10 personality disorders from Paranoid Personality Disorder to Obsessive-Compulsive Personality Disorder. To cover all the bases, there is an 11th category called Unspecified Personality Disorder for people who fall between the cracks of the categories and to keep the door open for something new that hasn't been seen before. We try to make diagnosing personality disorders as scientific as we can, but it is far from an exact science.

Dependent Personality Disorder

Jessica's personality style has a lot in common with Dependent Personality Disorder. You likely noticed her "enduring pattern" of dependency and submissive behavior. Not all of the items match her situation, but many of her ingrained patterns of thought, feeling, and behavior match the following criteria:

A pervasive and excessive need to be taken care of that leads to submissive and clinging behavior and fears of separation, beginning by early adulthood and present in a variety of contexts, as indicated by five (or more) of the following:

1. has difficulty making everyday decisions without an excessive amount of advice and reassurance from others
2. needs others to assume responsibility for most major areas of his or her life
3. has difficulty expressing disagreement with others because of fear of loss of support or approval (Note: Do not include realistic fears of retribution.)
4. has difficulty initiating projects or doing things on his or her own (because of lack of self-confidence in judgment or abilities rather than to a lack of motivation or energy)
5. goes to excessive lengths to obtain nurturance and support from others, to the point of volunteering to do things that are unpleasant
6. feels uncomfortable or helpless when alone, because of exaggerated fears of being unable to care for himself or herself
7. urgently seeks another relationship as a source of care and support when a close relationship ends
8. is unrealistically preoccupied with fears of being left to take care of himself or herself.[6]

---

6 American Psychiatric Association (2013). *Diagnostic and Statistical Manual: Mental Disorders* (rev. 5th ed.) Washington, D.C.: Author.

Are you still with me? Good. Now it's time for a little self-test. This test will look at your ingrained currents to see if they are contributing to the magnetic field attracting the Jerks. People who are Jerk Magnets or who may become a Jerk Magnet tend to:

- do things to please others even when they don't really want to
- feel responsible for the happiness of others
- want approval from others so they can feel good about themselves
- be unsure about their wants, desires, or needs
- want others to make decisions for them
- feel they are not good enough
- blame themselves when things aren't perfect
- feel like no one appreciates them
- have a big fear of rejection
- fear making mistakes or messing up
- try not to be too demanding on others
- easily make excuses for the failings of others
- think that others are better and smarter and know what's best for them
- feel that they can't take care of things by themselves
- spend a lot of time making sure others are happy and comfortable
- don't like being alone and get lonely easily
- try not to let their angry or hurt feelings show
- have a hard time getting close to others and are scared to trust others

- worry that people will leave them
- feel trapped in relationships
- cover up or lie for the people they love

Sound familiar? Now you may not have all of the above, but these thought, feeling, and behavior patterns are contributing to your side of the magnetic field. Like Jessica, you may not even be aware of how you began to have this personality style. Your story may be totally different from Jessica's, but the basic beliefs about yourself are probably similar. The Charged Particles of your early childhood and adolescence have combined to create your own "enduring pattern" of behavior which influences how you react to the world around you. These ingrained patterns likely have made you feel powerless and easily manipulated. Like Jessica, you may have become a powerless people pleaser.

Powerless People Pleaser

Without intending it, Jessica emerged from adolescence with a big need to be taken care of. Her low self-esteem, feelings of defectiveness, and need for approval from parents and others made her feel stuck. After she finished cosmetology school, she began styling hair at a local salon. She was good at her job, but as time went on she regretted leaving college. She decided to return to college and become a teacher. This was a big step for Jessica because she usually didn't make big decisions like this on her own. She was determined to reach her goal and was tired of doing what other people wanted.

Unfortunately, soon after she started college for the second time, she met the Jerk to end all Jerks. He was handsome and kind at first. What Jessica liked about him was that he was a leader. He was charming and smooth and the obvious leader of his small group of friends. For the first three months he was a "perfect gentleman." Since things were going so well, the Jerk proposed and Jessica accepted. Soon after the engagement, Jessica noticed the 180. He became demanding and angry. He would "flip out" at every little thing. He viewed Jessica as his property and would play on her insecurities to ensure he was in complete control of the relationship. He would disguise the control as a sign of his caring and wanting what was best for her. He was extremely jealous and said it was due to how much he loved her. The Jerk would frequently apologize for his angry outbursts and promise not to do it again.

Jessica learned from her early childhood to keep all negative thoughts, emotions, and feelings inside and did not tell her parents about how bad their relationship was. She desperately sought approval, especially from her mother and father. She didn't want them to know that things were going poorly. This made her really feel trapped, because she didn't want to be in the relationship with the Jerk, but at the same time wanted the approval of her parents. Things were bad. Jessica continued to retreat from any conflict, and began to feel more hopeless and depressed.

One night the Jerk and Jessica were watching a movie at home and he began to take off her clothes. Jessica was not in the mood and told him "no." He became very upset and began to hit and choke her. Jessica began crying and screaming, which woke her roommates. The Jerk was fuming and stormed out of the apartment. Jessica was terrified. While she had been emotionally abused and manipulated throughout her life, this was her first episode of physical abuse. She called her mother and told her what had happened.

Jessica's mother was shocked and went into rescuing-mother mode. Ever since Jessica was a little girl, her mother was there to protect and shelter her. Her mother saw Jessica as frail and helpless. Her mother drove all night and helped Jessica move out of her apartment, withdraw from school, and move back to the safety of her family's home. This relationship between Mother, Jessica, and the Jerk is what some experts call the Drama Triangle.[7]

The Drama Triangle

The three characters in the Drama Triangle are the Persecutor (Jerk), the Victim (Jessica), and the Rescuer (Mother).

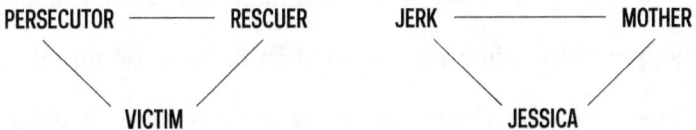

```
PERSECUTOR ——— RESCUER        JERK ——————— MOTHER
        \           /                  \            /
            VICTIM                        JESSICA
```

---

7 Karpman, Steven. 1968. "Fairytales and Script Drama Analysis," *Transactional Analysis Bulletin*. 7:39-43.

The basic idea behind the Drama Triangle is the power relationships between people. It is another way of looking at the roles people play in life and the way they see themselves in the world.

Victims feel oppressed, hopeless, helpless, and powerless. They generally feel overwhelmed and look to others to rescue them. They have a "poor me" attitude. Some people in life will play the victim role in every situation and even lie or inflate the situation so they can maintain the victim role.

A rescuer says, "I will help you." A rescuer can't help but rescue people and feels guilty if they don't rescue. Rescuers will help even if they are not asked to and will not even find out if the person wants to be helped. Rescuers don't mean to, but they keep the victim dependent. They are also known as enablers.

A perpetrator says, "It's your fault." Perpetrators blame and criticize. They are also rigid and can be authoritative. They keep the victim oppressed. Perpetrators sometimes feel that they are being persecuted and that they actually are the victim.

The reason it's called the Drama Triangle is that the people in the relationship are playing a role in a kind of subconscious script. Because Jessica's mother saw her daughter as frail and helpless, she did what she always had done, and came to Jessica's rescue. Because Jessica saw herself as defective and unable to make decisions, she put herself in the victim role. The Jerk was the perpetrator of the problem. The interesting thing about the Drama Triangle is that the roles being played can easily shift depending on your perspective. The Jerk actually felt like the victim because Jessica left without giving him a "second chance." From his perspective Jessica was the perpetrator of the problem. He saw her as running away from their relationship. By the time I started meeting with Jessica, she began to have guilt for leaving the Jerk. For some reason she had selective memory and only remembered the nice things he did for her at the beginning of the relationship. She doubted herself and second-guessed her decision. When she would voice her doubts to her parents they would "freak out." They would tell her how she was crazy if she went back to the Jerk and even forbid her from contacting him. After a while, her mother seemed like the persecutor, the Jerk was the victim, and Jessica was playing the rescuing role in defending the Jerk.

It is sometimes difficult to understand what is going on in our relationships. It is especially difficult to see the ingrained patterns when they have been there so long and become a part of who we are. Tools like the Drama Triangle try to describe human interaction in simple terms. This is all fine and good to identify personality styles and relation-ship dynamics, but you're probably thinking … so what? How can I use this information to help me stop being a Jerk Magnet? If you are thinking this, I'm glad. This means you are ready to move on to Chapter 5 when we start learning how to demagnetize.

CHAPTER FIVE

Demagnetize

So there's a magnetic field that's constantly attracting you to the wrong guy. Why is that? What is it about you, and what is it about the Jerk that causes the attraction? Let's review what we've learned so far. After reading about Players, *Mean*ipulators, and Psychopaths, you should feel confident in your ability to spot Jerks in their natural environment. Hopefully, you now have a better understanding of Jerks and it should be easier for you to avoid them in the wild. After reading about the Charged Particles of your life, you now know there are little parts of your personality that have combined to make you the person you are today. You learned a little about child development and attachment to see how the Charged Particles were formed in the first place. The previous chapter discussed the personality styles that are common in people who are Jerk Magnets. Now you're ready to start the demagnetization process.

Don't be so controllable

In the Jerk Spectrum chapter we learned that control was a big factor in how Jerks operate. For whatever reason, Jerks are controlling people and they are looking for people to control…the controllable. Nobody wants to think that they are easily controlled. Jessica believed that she had her own preferences and made up her own mind, but her personality style was one that looked to others to show her the way. One of Jessica's roommates told her later that she overheard the Jerk talking with his friend on his cell phone. "She's like my own puppet, I can get her to do or think whatever I want." Jessica was very upset when the roommate told her of this overheard conversation. As she looked back on their relationship she could see that the Jerk was slowly trying to control her the whole time. His main objective was to get her to be totally reliant upon him. He craftily separated her from her roommates; then he moved on to separate her from her family. His purpose was to have her all to himself and have complete power and control over her. How did she let this happen? Well, it was so subtle she didn't realize it was happening. As she reflected on her early attraction toward the Jerk, she mentioned that she liked his "take charge" attitude. He was a charming natural leader. After many sessions with Jessica, she was able to make the connection between her attraction to take-charge guys and how her father was a take-charge dad. She had always looked up to her father as a leader and a guy who "took care of the family." During her early childhood, this take-charge attribute was modeled for Jessica and she added it to her worldview of how the man is supposed to be. Fortunately for Jessica, her mother was able to stand up for her beliefs and views and was not dominated by Jessica's father.

Not every take-charge person is a Jerk, but pretty much every Jerk is a take-charge person (or at least wants you to think he is a take-charge person). Jessica was able to realize that she was looking for the ideal man, Mr. Right,

Mr. Just-like-Daddy. The problem was she wasn't just like Mommy. Her Charged Particles made it difficult for her to state a preference or take a stand. She felt defective. She felt that her views were stupid. This made her an easy target for the Players and *Mean*ipulators out there. They want people who are easily controlled. It's like keeping the front door to your house unlocked. Let's say there is a robber out there looking for an easy target. Usually the robber will scope out the area and identify homes that look promising. Let's say there are many homes on your street to choose from. If he tries a door and it's locked, sure, he can break in, but he is more likely to move on to the next house to find an open door. Jerks will scope you out too. They will check the door to see if you are controllable. If you offer some resistance and show that you are an independent, strong woman… sure, the Jerk can break in, but he will likely move on to the next easily controllable person.

How Jerks try the door

Early in your encounter with a Jerk, he will scope out your

thoughts. This may sound like the basic chit-chat of getting to know someone. He may ask you about your favorite things. What movies you like, what's the best this or that. What's better or who's hotter. What do you want to do or where do you want to go for dinner. This all sounds so innocent, but a Jerk is looking for someone that says a lot of "I don't know." Beware of the "I don't know." "I don't know" is different from "I don't care" or "I haven't really thought about that yet." "I don't know" is a sign to a Jerk that the door may be unlocked. A Jerk may interpret this as "I don't really want to say what I'm thinking because I want you to like me." Or, "I think I'm not too smart and you are so why don't you tell me."

Another way he may try the door is to see how much he can make you do. He may tell you what you should wear, how to do your hair, or how you should wear make-up. In another example, let's say a Jerk is sitting on the couch, and you are sitting on a chair across the room. A Jerk will say, "You should come over here and sit by me." This may be perfectly harmless for a regular guy. But for a Player or

*Mean*ipulator this is a control test. If you are the one to get up and sit by him, a Jerk may see this as the door being wide open.

Lock the door

Locking your door is easy to do. It's as simple as offering a little resistance and this may be all that is needed to send the message to a Jerk that you are not an easy target, that you are independent, strong, and *not* controllable. When you are in the chit-chat mode with someone (at this point he's just a regular guy and not a confirmed Jerk) be sure to take stands on things. It doesn't really matter what you say. The way to show that you are not a push over is to state a preference on things. Just don't say "I don't know," or "Wherever you want," because that signals to a Jerk a potential promising score. For example:

> Jerk: Where should we go to dinner?
> You: How about Zim's, I love their salsa.

Again, it's okay to say, "I don't really care," but in these early stages you need to take a stand.

So the Jerk is sitting on the couch and says, "You should come over here and sit by me." You say, "You should come over here and sit by me." I know this sounds silly, but remember, a Jerk decides if you are controllable during the early stages of the relationship. By offering signs of your independence and individuality, you show him you are not easily controlled, and if he wants a person like that, he should move on.

If you are in a relationship with someone who is not a Jerk, for sure it is okay to go and sit by him if he asks. In a relationship with mutual respect and understanding there is give and take. There is equality and love. Yes, that sounds good, but not for you...yet. You are in the process of demagnetizing and you'll have to make changes in your thoughts, feelings, and behavior in order to get those paper-clips off you.

Watch your need to please

We've seen how Jessica became trapped in her need to please others and how she interpreted the displeasure or disappointment of others as rejection and loss of love. As a Jerk Magnet, you likely are very aware of others' feelings. You probably go to great lengths to make sure people around you are happy. If people around you are unhappy, you somehow feel responsible. You may see pleasing people as a way of being accepted, and this helps you feel good about yourself. If you look into the Charged Particles of your past, there is probably a reason why this is so. Perhaps you had and angry or distant parent that was difficult to please and you made extra effort to be the perfect child in order to win your parent's love and affection. You may automatically think that if someone is unhappy it is your fault and like Jessica you equate unhappiness with rejection and love loss. You have become over-reliant on others and this over-reliance naturally leads you to want to please them.

Jerks will use and abuse your need to please up one side and down the other. Jerks know how to use your desire for security and attachment to their advantage. Remember Child Development Made Easy? Think of yourself as a caregiver with an emotional tie to a Jerk. The Jerk is able to get attention from you by dangling his mood in front of you like a carrot. Just like the infant who will cry, smile, cling, cuddle, and wave to get your attention and strengthen the bond, a Jerk will pout, yell, cry, and even threaten to get what he wants. As a Jerk Magnet, you put their needs and wants in front of yours because your Charged Particles make you interpret their unhappiness as rejection which make you feel abandoned, insecure, and alone.

Just because you like others to be happy and want to please others doesn't make you unusual. Most people like to please those around them. The way you will help demagnetize yourself is by observing your need to please. Be aware of when a Jerk is using his pleasure and acceptance as a prize to be won. Stop and ask yourself, "Why do I care so much if he is unhappy?" You may find there are basic beliefs about yourself that are driving the need to please. Hopefully, this awareness will help dissolve the connections between your need to please in order to feel good and the Jerks control over you with his bestowal of pleasure.

Make decisions for yourself

If the Charged Particles in your life have given you a view of yourself as weak, inadequate, or defective, it is natural for you to seek out others who will protect, care, and decide things for you; however, you need to make decisions for yourself. This is an expansion upon the theme of expressing your preference to show Jerks that you are a strong, independent individual and not a controllable target. This goes deeper in that you don't trust yourself to make good decisions. Again, this goes back to the Charged Particles of your personality. You may have come out of childhood and adolescence with a fear of messing up. You don't like making mistakes. Perhaps you messed up a lot as a kid and this was met with severe punishment or disappointment by those you were trying to please. You may have lost confidence in your ability to make choices and the thought of having to make decisions stresses you out. You automatically rely on others to make decisions for you to help you reduce your stress. You prefer that others take responsibility for the decisions in your life because your fear of failure is so great.

Because you feel weak and inadequate, you think others know what is best for you. You feel they are better or smarter.

Jessica constantly sought advice and reassurance from her family and friends before making decisions. As we looked at the patterns in her life, it became obvious that she basically did whatever her parents wanted her to do. Her parents advised her where to go to college, when to quit college and go to cosmetology school, etc. She wanted her parents to be happy with her and was a dutiful daughter. Her parents really wanted what was best for her and were there to support her emotionally and financially. She was lucky. Not all parents are that involved with their adult children's lives. Again, Jessica's parents (especially Mom) saw themselves in the Rescuer role. In their view, Jessica needed extra attention and consideration in order to be successful.

The first thing Jessica needed to do was decide what she really wanted. This was not easy to do. Jessica needed to carefully peel herself away from the hopes and dreams of her parents to discover what she wanted—what she truly desired deep down. Even though Jessica was an adult, she described her feelings regarding disappointing her parents as, "It's just like when I was a kid. My parents wanting me to do something, and me wanting to make them happy." Jessica was having difficulty breaking away from the attachment to her parents. She was stuck at a clingy and dependent stage in her emotional development, and her conflict between what she wanted and what other's wanted was increasing her feelings of powerlessness. The way we got down to her own true desire, which helped her make decisions for herself, was by playing "Why—Because."

Why—Because.

Why? Because. This is an annoying circular exchange I remember using as a kid when I didn't really have an explanation for my behavior. Someone (usually my parents) would ask me something like, "Why did you dump honey on your brother's head?" Answer: "Because." Parent: "Because, why?" Answer: "Just because." See, it's great... for a kid. As an adult, however, asking yourself why and then because can force you to look inward to help uncover the basic underlying beliefs you have about yourself. With Jessica, it was a way to peel herself away from the desires of her parents, friends, boyfriends, and fiancé to see what she wanted deep inside. Now we've already talked about saying "I don't know" and how this is the way many people avoid thinking about difficult or not-so-difficult issues. "I don't know" can easily become the default answer and signal to Jerks you may be controllable. For these reasons, "I don't know" is not allowed in Why—Because.

Me: Jessica, what do you really want to do with your life?
Jessica: I don't know.
Me: Beeeeeep. Sorry. I don't know is not allowed.
Jessica: I guess I want to do something to help others?
Me: Because. . .
Jessica: Helping others makes me feel good.
Me: Because. . .
Jessica: I don't know, uh, I mean, I guess my parents taught me that and it has been true for me in my life.
Me: Why is that?
Jessica: I guess I like feeling good.

Me: Sure. What can you do that will make you feel good?

Jessica: I always thought teaching kids would be fun?

Me: Because. . .

Jessica: You know, they're trying to learn and become something and I think it would feel good to help them.

Me: Because. . .

Jessica: Because, school was hard for me and I was able to make it so I think it will make me feel good to help them overcome their obstacles.

You're probably thinking, "This guy gets paid for this?" Well, it's true my job is relatively easy when you compare it with what Jessica is trying to work through to figure out why she has difficulty making decisions and why she relies on others so heavily. This is an exercise you can do to get to the heart of why there is a magnetic field attracting you to the wrong guy. It will help you identify basic beliefs about yourself. You first start with a statement like, "I'm pretty sure I'm a Jerk Magnet." Then just say to yourself, "Because…" and fill in the rest. "Because, only Jerks are attracted to me…Because…I let people walk all over me. Because…I don't feel like I deserve better…I want to be accepted…I hate feeling alone," etc. Who knows what will come out of this exercise, but what's important is that by doing this you eventually come to a basic understanding of yourself.

After doing the Why—Because statements with Jessica, she realized that what she really wanted to do was go back to school and become a teacher. She knew school would be difficult, but also knew this was something she really wanted for herself. Not to please anyone, not to be the dutiful daughter, but something she really wanted. We discussed that this goal could be difficult to achieve, and she may have some resistance from others. The important thing about Jessica's decision was that she came to this decision after a lot of introspection and made this decision on her own. I encouraged her to remember the feelings she had as she came to the conclusion that teaching was the thing that would make her the happiest. Remembering those strong feelings will help her in the future when she doubts whether or not her decision was the right one.

Don't be afraid to fail or succeed

Jerk Magnets sometimes feel that they are not as good as others. Sometimes they will not even make an attempt to succeed because they are afraid to fail. If you are afraid to fail you can use Why—Because statements to examine why failure is such an unacceptable thing. "I'm afraid to try to be successful because…if I don't succeed, people will think I'm an incompetent loser." "Failing is unacceptable because… it will prove that others are better and smarter than I am. I don't want the whole world to know how big of a loser I am…because, I really care what people think of me and I want to be seen as good." This is a most uncomfortable place to be and really epitomizes being stuck. You are afraid to win because if you were to win that goes against the underlying belief that you're not as good as others and messes up your worldview. Yes, success would be nice, but it's too risky. You are afraid to lose because that confirms your underlying belief and you don't need another confirmation of your established worldview.

In order to demagnetize, you must deal with your

fears. If fear is holding you hostage, it is time to lighten up and allow yourself the opportunity to succeed. If someone gives you a compliment, what's your first impulse? Shrug it off? Say, "No, it was nothing" or "they just feel sorry for me"? By doing this, you are minimizing someone's acknowledgement of your success. Don't be afraid to succeed. Say, "Thank you, I did work hard on that." You must recreate a world with a successful you in it. Allowing yourself the possibility of being successful is the first step in reshaping your worldview and will help to emotionally emancipate you from the oppressive fear of failure.

Stop fearing being alone

The fear of being alone may cause some Jerk Magnets to open the door to controlling Jerks. You may think, "I hate being alone," or "I need someone around me all the time to help me or in case something goes wrong." A Jerk may pick up on this theme. While he is scoping you out to see how controllable you are, he has a special "hate to be alone" sensor that is activated. Just as offering some initial resistance to the Jerk will likely send him on his way, when the "hate to be alone" sensor goes off the Jerk knows he's in business. He knows that you get lonely easier than other people and you are uncomfortable with the thought of being left to care for yourself. This thought may get you panicking about having to rely on your own resources and opens the flood gates of dependent submissive behavior.

This fear of being alone usually causes Jerk Magnets to stay in relationships with Jerks for long periods of time. Jerks will use this fear against you. It is one of the best weapons in their arsenal. Jerks will threaten to leave if you don't do what they want. An independent woman who doesn't fear being alone would say, "Fine, go." But a Jerk knows this fear will keep you bonded to him. He will try to separate you from your family and friends so he can become the sole provider of nurturance and support. If you find that you are in a relationship with a guy, and he is pitting you against your family or friends, and if you find that you are being asked to choose between the guy and your family/friends. Stop. Think. You are probably being controlled by your fear of being alone. "But we're in love, it's like forbidden love, like Romeo and Juliet." Okay, they both killed themselves in the big finale of that story. Not good.

Stop living defensively

If you are afraid to fail, you are probably living a careful defensive life. You don't like being in unfamiliar and uncomfortable situations. You feel secure with routine. Someone once said, "If you always do what you've always done, you'll always get what you've always gotten." And this is true when you are living the defensive life.

Jessica was living defensively by avoiding conflicts like the plague. She would quickly change the subject if she found that the subject matter was upsetting her Jerk. Conflict for Jessica meant a loss of love and support. She equated conflict with badness. If she ever got into a disagreement with someone, she would quickly give in even when she had valid reasons supporting her side of the argument. Her defensive strategies were conflict avoidance, and if she were to get into a conflict, quick conflict retreat. What does conflict mean to you? Badness? Pain? Disappointment? Disturbance of the peace?

The way Jessica learned to stop living defensively was to change the way she thought about conflict. Jessica viewed conflict as a battle. It was her will against his.

Thanks to the English language, we almost can't help but view an argument like a battle because most of the words we use to describe arguments have battle connotations. *Defend* your argument. *Attack* the weak points of their position. *Win* or *lose* the argument. Jessica found that if she thought of an argument or disagreement as a dance rather than a battle, she wouldn't feel the need to avoid or retreat from the dance. She tried to think of disagreements as two people with independent needs and wants working together to find a solution. There was give and take. There were no winners or losers. Sometimes she would follow, other times she would lead...a kind of conflict Cha-Cha. This change in her view of conflict helped her to release the negative feelings she had associated with disagreements and allowed her to stay and work out issues rather than retreat. You would think that the opposite of stop living defensively would be start living offensively. But no, it's just start living. In order to demagnetize, you have to do more than just think differently; you have to behave differently. Do things that you haven't always done. Challenge the automatic thoughts you have about yourself. Challenge the little voice in your mind that says, "Careful, you might fail and wouldn't that be embarrassing." Challenging the careful defensive life will take time and will feel uncomfortable at first. It's unpredictable and can be wild. But remember, the Charged Particles of your past are trying to dictate how you behave and react in the future. You can't change your past, but you can change the way you interpret the meaning of the past. By challenging the careful defensive life, you begin to break the ingrained thoughts, feelings, and behaviors that are invisibly attracting you to Jerk after Jerk.

Be more independent.

Jerk Magnets sometimes have difficulty showing initiative or being independent. Why is that? You guessed it, all the things we have been talking about: Fear of failure, defensive "safe" living, not wanting to displease others, fear of rejection, fear of being alone, etc. If you're a person who has difficulty showing initiative or being independent, saying, "Be more independent" won't help. It's like saying, be taller. You want to be more independent, it's just scary and you may feel it's impossible. With some fears it is common practice to be exposed to the fear a little bit at a time. If you are afraid of heights, a therapist may tell you to begin desensitizing yourself by first looking at a ladder. Then over time, putting your foot on the first rung and then stepping down. Bit by bit you become more comfortable with height and you are better able to tolerate the uncomfortable feelings. You still may be afraid of heights, but your ability to tolerate the height has improved.

If you're the kind of person who doesn't like being alone, being independent is difficult and causes you great anxiety. Like the person who is afraid of heights, a step-by-step approach is needed to help you become more comfortable with being independent. The step-by-step approach that I used with Jessica was the Decide, Plan, Follow Through.

Decide, Plan, Follow Through

Jessica's ability to make decisions, plan, and follow through had been weakened because of years of insecurity and dependence on others. She had no confidence in her ability to succeed. Her skills at communicating her own ideas were weak and because of her conflict avoidance and retreat pattern, she was terrible at resolving conflicts. The Why— Because exercise helped Jessica decide what she really wanted to do with her life and why she wanted to do it. She made the decision to be a teacher. Now what? For Jessica this was a big step because she usually doubted her ability to make the right decision. She needed to get away from such big picture issues as Right with a capital R and just focus on what was right with a small r for her now in her life.

The next step for Jessica was to make a plan. She thought about her different educational options and decided it would be best to go to another college about one hour north of her home. She investigated the program and found that many of her credits transferred and she could finish in less than two years. She told her parents of her strong desire to become a teacher and they were impressed by her newfound direction in life. They sensed her conviction and said they would help her any way they could. (They also wanted to get her further away from the Jerk.) It sounds like everything was perfect, right? Not so fast. Jessica's doubts began to creep in. Her Charged Particles of the past were making her remember her old worldview. Her incorrect basic beliefs that she was defective and unable to make good decisions made her return to her insecure ways.

This is where it gets tricky—the follow through part. It seems like this is the snag with everyone, Jerk Magnet or not. We get great ideas of how we're going to change this or start up that. There's emotion and energy but then, after the emotion has gone away and time goes by, the follow through part is what keeps us from the goal. To help give Jessica the conviction to follow through with her plan, I asked her to remember the feeling she had when she came to the conclusion that teaching was her deep down desire. She described it as an "excitement and energy" that was cheering her on toward her goal. I told her that when her feelings of fear and needing to rely on others crept in, she was to close her eyes and remember this excitement and energy feeling. It seems like a simple thing, but the feeling she had when she came to the conclusion about what to do with her life is the foundation of her independence and self-confidence. This remembrance would be the calm reassurance that she is doing what was right for her. Despite having some doubts, she followed through, enrolled in school, and began the journey towards becoming a teacher.

Okay. Good for Jessica. What about you? To help in the demagnetization process, you must start small, and practice a step-by-step process of deciding, planning, and following through. Why? Because. It's out with the old, in with the new. This is how to increase your independence and build confidence in your ability to feel, think, and do things on your own. Decide on something, plan it out, and then do it. Redecorate the apartment, organize the closet, take a pottery class, start an exercise program, learn to play the guitar, or the accordion (with proper supervision of course…accordions can be dangerous in the wrong hands). Then, give yourself credit when you successfully decide, plan, and follow through with something. You are reshaping your worldview with an independent you in it—a you that can get things done. Your ability to be more independent will increase with each successful venture. You will begin to live. No careful defensive life here. You're doing your own thing, the right thing for you. Without even realizing it, you will be strengthening your assertiveness muscles, making you a stronger person. A Jerk will see you doing your own thing and keep walking down the street to find an easy unlocked Jerk Magnet's door.

✎ TAKE HOME MESSAGE #4

In order to demagnetize, you have to do more than just think differently; you have to behave differently. Do things that you haven't always done. Challenge the automatic thoughts you have about yourself. Beware the safe defensive life. Start living.

CHAPTER SIX

Guy Jerk Magnets and Female Jerks

For the majority of this book, it has been assumed that the Jerks in the world from Player to Psychopath are male and the Jerk Magnets are female. While this may be true for the majority of people I see in my practice, there are a healthy number of Guy Jerk Magnets out there who fly under the radar. This is likely due to the core differences between men and women. If you survey the psychiatrists of the world, you would find that for all psychological issues a greater number of women seek therapy as compared to men. Why? Who knows? Perhaps men are more hesitant to admit they have a problem and are more reluctant to talk with someone about their issues. This doesn't necessarily mean there are fewer depressed men out there than women. Perhaps it is a societal thing. Men are supposed to be strong, macho, provider-protectors. Being vulnerable and sensitive are not the qualities of maleness promoted in beer commercials. Admitting to someone that you are easily manipulated by women, also, doesn't help your ego. A look into a Guy Jerk Magnet's life may help illustrate the complex issues.

Jared's Story

Jared was twenty-seven and unhappy. He desperately wanted a relationship and was paralyzed by social situations. Jared never knew his father and for the first five years of his life he lived on a ranch in Texas with his mother, who worked as a riding instructor. Jared recalls that there were many adults on the ranch who gave him attention, and he had a great feeling of security and love. This all changed when his mother changed careers and moved to Oklahoma City to become a beautician. He was now left alone while his mother worked, and he reports that his mother stopped hugging him during this time. He reported, "My mother never gave me or taught me about affection and now I have no idea how to get close to anyone." With his mother working, Jared was left alone and was mostly entertained by watching T.V. He said that he was "terrified by kids in school and was always picked on." During these years, he found that he was a good storyteller and developed a habit of lying to the other kids. He told them that he was really royalty from England and that his dad was a long-lost heir to the English throne. Another one was that his real dad was a CIA operative and was living in Europe collecting information.

This is a very common fantasy for children who feel they have been abandoned. They frequently make up stories about their true identity and hold to the wish that someday their loved ones will come to rescue them. Jared's dad never did. As the years progressed, Jared became so good at lying his lies sometimes became true to him. Even though he never played sports, he would tell women that he was captain of his high school football team and played semi-pro football until he hurt his back. He would talk of fights he had been

in where he defended the honor of women. He was a hero…
in his eyes.

Many of Jared's issues are similar to Jessica's. He indeed
had a low self-esteem, but it was not because he felt defective. He felt abandoned by his mother and blamed her for
his inability to socialize with women. Because he felt abandoned as a child, he developed a persistent fear that he would
be abandoned by women in the future. This fear caused him
to over idealize the romantic relationship. Whenever he met
a girl, instead of just enjoying her company and learning
more about her, he would immediately jump the gun and
start thinking about marriage. He wore his emotions on his
sleeve. These Charged Particles combined to set him up for
problems with women. For one thing, any regular girl would
quickly realize that he was clingy or "over emotional," and
would leave before a relationship even started. This left his
door wide open for manipulative women to enter and drain
his bank account.

When he was twenty-one he met Leticia, his first "girl-
friend." They would go to the mall together and Leticia

would get Jared to buy her things. He said they never kissed and never even really went out on a real date. Leticia never wanted to introduce Jared to her friends or family. Sound familiar? A female Player? Why not? At age twenty-five he met Jorgia, a single mom with two kids. He loved her kids and remembers that Jorgia would use the kids to get Jared to buy things for the family. He bought them school clothes, paid for their rent and cable. Jared and Jorgia rarely went out and if Jared ever questioned where Jorgia was, who she was with, or what she was doing, she would threaten to break up with him. After a while, threatening to break up began to lose its power over Jared, and that's when she began to threaten suicide. Ah, the ultimate abandonment. "I don't know what I would do to myself if you don't _____." (Fill in the manipulative blank.)

Jared became terrified of relationships with women, and began to see himself as an awkward loner. He would try to talk with women, but as the years went by, he became more and more uncomfortable in social situations. He got to the point that he wouldn't talk to women at all, or if he did need to talk with a women (let's say in a department store), he would seek out older women. It's interesting that he felt more comfortable with women in their 50's and 60's. This, perhaps, goes back to his early childhood and his desire for the warmth and comfort he received from his mother before she stopped hugging him. He has become emotionally stuck at this early level of development. Jared's relationships are now superficial and he has lost confidence in his ability to even have a relationship with someone.

The core issues that make one a Jerk Magnet can be applied to both men and women. Men also have Charged Particles of childhood and adolescence that combine to create an enduring pattern of behavior that influences how they react to the world. They can be every bit as afraid of being alone, or of messing up, or of being rejected as women can be. The important issue of this chapter is to highlight some of the societal challenges that face the Guy Jerk Magnet that need to be taken into consideration for his demagnetization process.

Macho, macho man myth

From a very young age, boys and girls are taught by their parents, the media, and other children, how they should behave. Society sends strong messages to boys that they must be strong, tough, and assertive. Boys are told, "Be a man." If they are not strong and assertive, they are viewed as "sissies" and shunned by other boys. Boys are encouraged to be aggressive and are even rewarded for it. On the athletic field, they are expected to excel, and if they are not good at sports, they are insulted by, "You throw like a girl." Society sends a clear message that it is natural for boys to be more physical and competitive. "Boys will be boys."

On the other hand, girls are taught they should be passive, shy, and quiet. They are to be nurturers and the caretakers of others. Men are expected to keep emotions inside and not openly express their feelings. Society tells the guy how he's supposed to be: tough, confident, in control. Society even tells the guy what he should and shouldn't like. It probably begins in our early childhood. If you think about the advertising you saw on Saturday morning T.V. as a kid, you'll remember toys targeted to boys and girls in different ways. Robots, cars, action figures for boys; Barbies, Ponies, stuffed animals for girls. This served to reinforce the stereotypical roles for boys and girls, men and women. As adults, we are told what sexy is or isn't, what we should drive, wear, eat, and who is desirable. Nowhere are the stereotypical male and female roles more apparent than in the romantic relationship. Men are expected to make the first move, ask the women out, pay for the date, ask women to dance, etc. They are to be active, never passive. While times are changing, and more women now ask men out, they can be considered forward, and may be viewed as intimidating. What is forward and intimidating for the women to do is expected behavior for the man. This can put a lot of pressure on a guy.

The pressure became too much for Jared, and after many unsuccessful relationships, he became reclusive and escaped into a virtual world of video games and online communities. This was a safe place for him to re-create himself into the person he really wished he could be. He had many "friends" around the world who only knew him under the terms he controlled. This is where the lying skills he had honed as a youth really came in handy. Today Jared lives alone and spends most of his evenings and nights online. He wishes he could have a relationship with a real woman, but his fear of being used and abandoned holds him captive.

Demagnetize

The same principles apply to men and women in the demagnetization process. Men also need to not be so controllable, watch their need to please, make decisions for themselves, stop fearing being alone, be independent, and not fear failure. People are people after all and the underlying personality style that allows you to enter into relationships with Jerks will be similar for men and women. It is critical that you examine the basic beliefs about yourself to uncover what your Charged Particles are and what happened in your life to make them charged. Why—Because can be helpful in this area. With Jared, it went like this:

Me: Jared, why is it so hard for you to talk with women?

Jared: Probably because I'm afraid they will make fun of me or laugh.

Me: Why do you think that?

Jared: Because that's what usually happens or they just ignore me.

Me: Why would they do that?

Jared: Because I get real nervous and lose my confidence.

Me: Because…

Jared: I've never felt confident around girls.

Me: Because…

Jared: They scare me.

Me: Because…

Jared: Well, it seems like whenever I get close to someone or give them my heart, they end up not liking me.

Me: Why is that?

Jared: I guess I'm unlikable and will never have a real relationship.

Jared's basic belief of being unlikable was closely tied to his feeling of rejection and abandonment by his mother. We discussed how this feeling was causing him to behave in a clinging, dependent way and setting him up to be used by Jerks.

Challenges for the Guy Jerk Magnet

Because of society's myth of the Macho Man and the stereotypical gender roles and behavior for men and women, Jared's reaction to being a Jerk Magnet is common. Jessica's response to the Charged Particles of her past was to become a Powerless People Pleaser. Because of the stereotypical gender roles society encourages, it was socially acceptable for her to be more passive and "wait for the right guy to come along." Unfortunately, her personality style was paving the way for Jerks to walk right in. Society expects Jared to "be a man," "wear the pants," and not "act like a woman." He must be the instigator, the pursuer, and the aggressor. Because of Jared's past and basic beliefs, he was easily manipulated by Jerks which caused him to retreat from the "dating game." In a society where you are expected to do the asking out, if you stop asking, you will most likely be alone.

There are generally two scenarios for the Guy Jerk Magnet. Number one is what happened to Jared. He got burned several times, which caused him to fear women. He retreated into a world of social isolation and re-created himself in the virtual world. People with personality styles like Jared's fear disapproval, criticism, and rejection. They view themselves as socially inept, ugly, or inferior to others. They create a safe and secure isolated world for themselves where they can fantasize they are confident, smooth, and in control.

The second scenario is also fairly common—the Guy Jerk Magnet who gets stuck married to a Jerk. His Charged Particles have caused his self-esteem to be extremely low. He has lost his confidence, seeks the approval of others to feel good about himself, fears abandonment and rejection, and has difficulty making decisions. Somehow, he gets married to a manipulative woman and becomes a "beaten-down man." He is similar to the millions of women who are married to controlling, chauvinistic, domineering men. Society looks upon him as "not wearing the pants" or being a "wimp." He doesn't make decisions for his family, and he is unable to stand up to his controlling wife. In order to control him, a manipulative wife will threaten to harm him, his possessions, his pets, herself, or even the children. She may condition her love and affection upon his doing what she wants. The Guy Jerk Magnet is so afraid of what she may do (or not do), he passively complies to her wishes. His Charged Particles cause him to intensely fear being alone and to feel guilt when others are unhappy. Like Jessica, he may indeed be stuck at an earlier level of emotional development, which causes him to remain stuck in his adult relationship. He also may begin to lie to others regarding his past accomplishments, and inflate his abilities in an effort to re-create himself in a world where he feels more accepted in society. He also is liable to try and escape the relationship, not physically, but emotionally and mentally, by immersing himself in work, school, hobbies, his children's lives, video games, or online communities.

Okay, this is a bonus test for you men out there who may be a Guy Jerk Magnet, or those readers who know and love someone who may be. In addition to the items listed in the previous chapter to describe regular Jerk Magnets, people who are Guy Jerk Magnets or who may become Guy Jerk Magnets tend to:

- Live their life as a victim of circumstance
- Have difficulty taking responsibility for their actions and tend to easily blame others for their short comings
- Have a high tolerance for emotional pain
- Tell "tall-tales" which is a nice way of saying they lie easily and are good at it
- Have poor memories of their past mistakes and the mistakes of others
- Keep busy so they don't have to think about things
- Not get much joy out of things and have difficulty having fun
- Let others hurt them without trying to protect themselves
- Keep their emotions inside and don't need anything from anyone
- Feel powerless to change their situation

Society can be harsh and does not look upon weakness favorably, especially if you are perceived as a weak man. I think this is why the Guy Jerk Magnet attempts to cope with his ingrained patterns of behavior in an escapist way. Lying can be an escape. Isolation is an escape. Living up to the societal and cultural norms of being confident, in control, and assertive, can be overwhelming to someone with basic beliefs that they are unlikable, not good enough, and weak.

For a guy, the important moments of his life and things he uses to define who he is in the world are greatly influenced by the societal and cultural values and norms. By not fitting into the societal mold, he feels isolated and "different" from the others, which further knocks down his self-esteem. These influences may not necessarily increase his magnetic pull to the wrong person, but definitely influence the way he copes with relationships and with people in general. He is more likely to have anxiety and depression. He may feel compelled to excessively work, eat, drink alcohol, or use drugs, even when he doesn't get much enjoyment out of these activities. Life is not easy for the Jerk Magnet, and because of societal pressure, it is especially difficult for the Guy Jerk Magnet.

CHAPTER SEVEN

Teenage Jerk Magnets and the Family

Many of Jessica's Charged Particles (stuff that happened to shape her self-esteem and worldview) began in adolescence and contributed to the Electric Currents (ingrained pattern of thought, feeling, or behavior) that caused her to become a Jerk Magnet as an adult. It is important to understand that the early teenage years are critical in identifying and preventing the ingrained patterns that lead to becoming a Jerk Magnet.

I have worked with hundreds of teenage girls with malnourished emotional development and I noticed they had several things in common. If I were to pinpoint the age when their problems with attachment, bonding, and security seem to manifest—it would be with the start of adolescence. Case after case showed a relatively healthy, happy, confident child from toddler age up to about age 12. Right at 7th to 8th school grade (in the United States) is when things start to go downhill for some children. The likely reason is that the biological and emotional changes that occur during this time can be stressful and embarrassing. Teenagers may become overly sensitive; likely they feel uncomfortable and are sensitive about their physical appearance. They are irritated easily, lose their temper often, and may feel depressed. To add to the joy, they can start to have extreme changes in mood or mood swings. They can feel confident and happy one second, then irritated and depressed in a short span of time. These mood swings are likely due to shifting levels of hormones. Their brains are also continuing to mature and develop, and their physical bodies will mature faster than their brains. The behavior we tolerated when they were five or seven (tantrums or crying) is now annoying to us when they are thirteen. We may find ourselves telling them to "grow up" because we are tricked in to thinking they are older than they really are, or at least their outward appearance seems older. They can be more logical and communicate better, yet their brains and emotional development are still, well, in development.

The timing of puberty is an important thing to be aware of as a parent. It can be an indicator of either positive or negative things to come. Researchers have found that the timing of puberty can have significant effects on a teenager's self-esteem. Boys that mature later can have more feelings of personal inadequacy, rejection, and may feel dominated by others. Boys that mature early are found to be more self-confident, independent, and play a more mature role in social relationships. Girls who mature early are at greater risk for depressive and anxiety symptoms and are also more likely to develop delinquent behavior. Girls that mature later are more competent, responsible, adaptable, and are found to function at a higher level in school. So while we may not have any control over when puberty occurs, it is important to be educated about the conditions that occur with early onset of puberty in girls and late onset of puberty in boys.

Quest for identity

Early teenage years are additionally tough because on top of all these moving parts, there is the quest for identity and individualization, which is the all-important goal of development. During the teenage years, kids begin to get a sense of who they are—their individual identity. For teenagers, this is big. It becomes extremely important for a teenager to feel they are a unique individual, but not too unique. Being the loner can be lonely. It's more comfortable to find a friend or small group of friends that share your likes, dislikes, style, and opinions. As most parents will attest, the friends of the teenager become the most important things in their life. They have a powerful influence on the teen and again, this is a normal process in development.

During this time, the body is maturing sexually and a teenager will become more curious and interested in sex. Developing a sexual identity is an important part of the developmental process and can be some of the most highly Charged Particles there are. Early maturing girls will find they get more attention from boys, especially older boys—

which can become a problem. For one thing, they quickly learn that they can get all kinds of attention by being sexual with boys. If a young girl with low self-esteem now has boys showing interest in her if she will text inappropriate pictures of herself to them—what will she do? She will start sending pictures of herself.

One fourteen year old I worked with sent topless pictures of herself to her classmates because "they would tell me I was pretty." This is the perfect example of early development of the body and late development of the brain. Now that she is seventeen, she better understands how "stupid" she was and that the boys didn't really care about her. Of course, at age fourteen, she "knew it all" according to her parents, and couldn't see how the choices she was making weren't in her best interest in the long run. I find this Mark Twain quote amusing because it is so true. "When I was a boy of fourteen, my father was so ignorant I could hardly stand to have the old man around. But when I got to be twenty-one, I was astonished by how much he'd learned in seven years." Unfortunately, the brain continues to mature and develop until about age 25—so sometimes the adolescent ride can be long and bumpy. When young people push the boundaries of their upbringing, I explain to parents the process of child development and let them know that it is a predictable part of the process. The difficult part as a parent is knowing which battles to choose and which to let go. If you can weather the storm, the child will usually come to a point when they realize they don't know it all, and they will be astonished by how much you have "learned in seven years." It is essential to have conversations with your child about sex and sexuality. Some researchers believe these conversations should start as early as age eight and they should happen often. If you don't lay down the boundaries of what is appropriate and inappropriate behavior and attitudes, you will allow the media, YouTube, or their peers to educate them. A big part of the conversation is helping the child understand the idea of "natural consequences" for behaviors. Kelly found out the hard way about natural consequences.

Kelly, at age 15, found out that she developed a reputation of being a "slut" when she had sex with her seventeen-year-old boyfriend. Many of her female friends at school rejected her because of this. She began to get unwanted attention from many more boys. She changed schools, but the reputation followed and she again began getting unwanted attention. Kelly's Charged Particles made her feel uncomfortable when she was alone, and she used her sexuality to get attention from boys at her new school. She, unfortunately, misinterpreted their interest in her sexually and found it didn't extend to interest in her as a person. She began to feel more alone, unwanted, and abandoned. Her relationships became more and more dramatic, volatile, and she began to have more Players and *Mean*ipulators than she ever wanted.

Sexual Identity

Another aspect of the quest for identity and the developmental task of feeling separate and independent is sexual identity. I've worked with many young girls from highly religious homes who declare with impunity that they are bisexual or lesbian or pansexual (open to relationships with people who do not identify as strictly men or women). I can tell that their sexual orientation is the button they push with parents that is sure to get their attention (usually negative). When I talk with them about their sexuality—and they tell me about their orientation that goes against their particular religious values—I can tell they are using it as a litmus test to see if I will judge them or treat them differently. I find I have been most effective in creating a relationship with them if I am interested in them as a person and not as a label based on their sexuality. Once they feel I am not judging them, we can move forward with the process of identifying personality patterns that lead them into unhealthy relationships. It seems like parents get sucked into the drama of their child's proclaimed sexual identity, which then gets over-emphasized in the overall picture of a child's development. Parents seem to worry about how their child's orientation or identity will affect them as parents and how they will be judged rather than work to develop an honest, loving, and non-controlling relationship with their child. Sometimes children will use their proclaimed sexual identity as a smoke screen or decoy to avoid talking about other more important relationship issues. Once parents can help their child feel like they are not judging them, they can move forward with the relationship. The good news is that once teenagers achieve separation and develop their own identity, things will stabilize and they will be better able to develop love relationships and achieve mastery over their body impulses—but it does take patience and time.

Identification and Prevention

The same basic principles apply to identifying the Charged Particles and Electric Currents that contribute to becoming a Jerk Magnet for a teen as it is for an adult. The context of the social interactions may be slightly different and the good news is, if you can identify these patterns in their beginning stages, the behavior and brain can be guided and changed to lessen the chance they will turn into a Jerk Magnet.

Jessica emerged from childhood with low self-esteem, desperately sought approval from others, felt like she had little control, and with feelings of low levels of security.

What could her parents have done to identify some of these thoughts and behaviors early on? Here are some questions for parents.

- Does your teen go to desperate lengths to fit in?
- Do they sacrifice the things they want to let others have their way?
- Are they easily bossed around by others?
- Do they have to ask everyone else's opinion before they can make a decision?
- Are they always looking for reassurance?
- Do they go to extreme efforts to not have to be alone?
- Are they big-time conflict avoiders?
- Does your teen have difficulty expressing disagreement for fear of loss of friends?
- Do they defend their friends even when they know their friends are wrong?
- Do they let others dictate how they feel and act?

Unfortunately, Jessica's parents did not appreciate the person Jessica was becoming. They couldn't know of her desperate need to please others and her loss of her sense of who she was. If these items are present in your child's thoughts and behaviors, these are early warning signs of becoming a Jerk Magnet.

Nip it in the bud.

Obviously, nip it in the bud is a saying that means to put an end to something before it develops into something larger (cut off the part that develops into a flower before it blooms). But I want you to think of it in a slightly different way. We have a peach tree that seldom ever produces fruit. One year we had tons of buds and we were very excited to have peaches galore. My brother-in-law (who is what I would call a guru of gardening) told me it was important to pull off some of the buds so the tree could focus on developing fewer peaches. This way, the peaches that remained would be larger, healthier, and this would be better than having tons of small, poorly developed peaches. We followed his advice, thinned out the buds, and were happy with the peach extravaganza.

So how does a well-meaning parent nip some of these thoughts, feelings, and behaviors once they are identified. If you think of the peach-tree metaphor, you can identify some of the core issues such as low self-esteem or low self-confidence and focus on developing those aspects—

the core issues, rather than focus on behaviors that occur because of the core issues.

Rachel was a thirteen-year-old girl "addicted" to her phone. She would spend all of her free time on social media sites messaging and texting to the exclusion of her family. Her parents, in frustration, would take away her media privileges often because that seemed to be the only thing that would get her attention. This would cause her to feel depressed, and she would isolate herself more. The parents were caught in a Drama Triangle where they were the Persecutors, Rachel was the Victim, and she used her friends on social media as the Rescuers. Once Rachel's parents realized what was happening in this situation, they changed their tactics. They started to realize that historically, they would only reward Rachel when she did things to please them, which trained her to be a pleaser. They also realized that in their family they bottled up emotion and were not good at expressing emotions—especially negative emotions. They started with a new family rule that it was okay to allow yourself to feel angry, scared, or lonely, and it was okay to say so. They worked on modeling behavior of "owning" their own feelings and not blaming their feelings on someone or something else. They also started to reward Rachel for independent acts and times when she would take initiative—more focus on her process than her outcome.

Studies have shown that focusing on the outcome and labeling rather than focusing on the process can cause increased anxiety and loss of confidence in your child. If you say to your child, "You're so smart," you may think this is a good thing. Your goal is to have children view themselves as smart and feel good. However, if "smartness" becomes too central to the identity of a child, when the day comes they do something dumb or they learn they are not the smartest, they can be devastated. The reality goes against their basic belief, and they become timid, scared, and are afraid to try new things. Rachel's parents found it was more helpful to focus on the process, "Rachel, you're such a hard worker," or "Rachel, you really didn't give up."

Now this process wasn't easy; it took time, but Rachel began to lose her Electric Current that she was "not good enough." This ingrained thought that she was not good enough had caused her to seek out support from social media, friends, and contributed to her fear of being alone. Thanks to her parents' change in focus and behavior, she no longer needed reassurance from everyone, and was able to take more responsibility for her behavior and her decisions.

It is important to understand that many of Rachel's behaviors and her "phone addiction" were secondary to the core issues of low self-esteem, poor self-confidence, and not owning her feelings. If her parents just focused on her behaviors and "nipping" those secondary behaviors, the buds would just continue to emerge over time. Her parents wisely were able to thin out her core issues, understanding the connection to the unwanted/addictive behaviors, and allowed her to focus on developing the parts of her personality that would help her become a more healthy person overall.

You might be creating a Teenage Jerk Magnet if...

If you have identified aspects of your child that match up with the beginning stages of becoming a Jerk Magnet, the next step is to help them demagnetize and take steps to prevent more Jerk Magnet traits from emerging. Like Jessica's parents had to learn, and Rachel's parents figured out— they, as parents, played a part in the creation of their child's self-esteem and confidence. Many times parents don't even realize the messages they are sending their children, and it can take an objective third party (counselor or therapist) to help them see the patterns of Charged Particles that are combining to create a Jerk Magnet.

Like Rachel's parents, do you give rewards for pleasing others and no rewards for independent acts? Do you allow a dependency upon rewards for self-esteem? Do you support the development of personal boundaries? Do you make most of the decisions for your child or do you let them have a say? One of the chief complaints I get from Teenage Jerk Magnets is that of controlling, dominating, and perfectionistic parents. Sometimes parents have such anxiety that they can't tolerate allowing their children to make their own decisions—especially if the children potentially are going to fail. Many parents are rescuers and enable their children to not take responsibility for their decisions. Take the example of Jana: If Jana ever had an opinion that went against her mother's view, her mother would attribute the new attitude to whomever was Jana's newest or closest friend. Rather than acknowledge the poor decision making ability and responsibility of her daughter, Jana's mother would blame Jana's friends when Jana broke curfew. Her mother would blame the teacher, school, or even the test as being unfair if Jana did poorly.

The message was clear, it is always someone else's fault. This family pattern made it difficult for Jana to have a voice in the family or have confidence in her ability to make decisions for herself. Jana developed the need to have others take responsibility and had little confidence in her own abilities. This training and void in a person's personality creates the perfect environment for a Jerk to step in. If a person feels like they are not capable of making good decisions, a Player or *Mean*ipulator will gladly make decisions for them and hold their approval out as the reward.

As you can see, there are many factors and variables that can contribute to the creation of a Teenage Jerk Magnet. I don't think I can overstate the impact social media and constant contact with peers through texting and messaging can have on the nervous system of developing adolescents. It seems that the immediacy of the feedback and the potential for anonymous bullying causes significant anxiety and it promotes more isolative behavior. I have worked with many children described as "addicted" to electronics, and it is important for parents to educate their children on how to have healthy limits and boundaries on electronic communication and interaction. Once family patterns and evidence of emotional malnutrition can be identified in their beginning stages, the behavior and brain can be guided and changed to lessen the chance they will turn into a Jerk Magnet.

TAKE HOME MESSAGE #5

Parents can identify Jerk Magnet traits early in brain development and "nip them in the bud" in order to help their child own their emotions, understand natural consequences of behavior, and get fulfillment from the process rather than the outcome.

CHAPTER EIGHT

Change of Brain

Like any self-help process, it is easy to know what you are "supposed" to do and quite another thing to apply the newly learned skills. How many folks out there know exactly how to lose weight, have even researched out the most successful methods, only to continue to struggle with ingrained eating habits and failure to lose weight? Billions of dollars are spent every year on the diet industry—and most diets do have short-term results. Unfortunately, unless there is a lifestyle change, the majority of people will regain their weight once they stop dieting. How many people have addictive behaviors or other habits they know they need to stop, but can't seem to maintain the energy and emotion necessary to make a lifestyle change? You've heard of someone having a change of heart? If applied, the skills learned in this book will help you to actually have a change of brain.

The emerging understanding of neuroplasticity is exciting and gives a nice biological and chemical explanation to what therapists and behavioralists have been doing for decades. Neuroplasticity refers to changes in neural pathways due to changes in behavior, environment, thinking, and emotions. For many years, it was thought that after a certain point of development, the brain was unchangeable. Now we know that new connections can be made. This is the biological explanation for how a thought can become a behavior, which when repeated can become a habit, which can become a lifestyle.

Near my home is Mount Timpanogos—a beautiful mountain that towers over all other mountains in the area at 11,752 feet. As the sun sets in the west, a beautiful orange glow is cast on the impressive limestone and dolomite rock to the east of the Utah Valley. As you look to the top of Mount "Timp," you can see little rivulets from melting snow that turn into larger fissures and crevices that coalesce to form mighty canyons at the base. How did those canyons form? From the tiny rivulets of water taking the same path down the mountain for years and years, eroding away the rock and dirt to eventually form the canyon. The water just follows gravity and takes the most direct path down. This is like your brain. Your brain is like Mount Timp, and your thought patterns are the "rivulets" or connections that form neural pathways.

The Charged Particles (your past and personality that shape you) that led to the Electric Currents (ingrained patterns of thoughts and behavior) are biologic rivulets that create canyons of fixed belief, self-identity, and habits. So, because of the ingrained patterns or neural path, it is very difficult to change the behavior and automatic thoughts. To actually change, real change, a change to the core, the brain connection/current/rivulet has to change. A new pathway down the mountain has to be created. This is what is happening with therapy—changing the way the brain is connected or changing the pathway. Yes, you heard that right. Changing patterns of thought, over time, repeatedly, will change the actual physical connections in your brain. So by using the demagnetization skills learned in Chapter 5, you will, over time, change how your brain is connected. The new connection will mean that the previous automatic thoughts, feelings, and even behaviors will be "re-wired" to enable you to respond to the old situations in a new way.

Now the brain doesn't really like to change—as you know. Those pathways are pretty fixed. Jessica's pathways were fixed by keeping her thoughts, emotions, and feelings inside, seeking approval from others, and avoiding conflict—which led to her inability to stand up for herself. The rivulets in childhood and adolescence eventually turned into canyons—which equaled, you guessed it, Jerk Magnet. Rachel's pathways manifested by her "phone addiction" were secondary to the core issues of low self-esteem, poor self-confidence, and not owning her feelings. Again, leading to Jerk Magnetism.

In Jessica's life, she started to work on being more independent. She decided on a plan to study secondary education and re-enrolled in school to finish her bachelor's degree. It was difficult for her to stay focused as she remembered all the core issues driving her to please others. We had to work hard on overcoming her fear of failure. I had her imagine making lesson plans for her students, visualize herself teaching in front of students, and when she would get discouraged, remind herself that this is something she wanted, independent of anyone else.

The process of changing the path of Jessica's brain was left with one last hurdle: overcoming her negative thinking. Many times, Jessica's negative thinking would sabotage her plans. She understood her Charged Particles had shaped her perception of reality, but still had a hard time re-shaping it. We understood why she thought the way she did. She improved in many ways, but the automatic negative thoughts were the last thing to go. Negative thinking is very common for people who struggle with Jerk Magnetism. It's like there is a negative mind processor that transforms all incoming data into the most negative interpretation possible. For example, if someone would give Jessica a compliment, she would automatically think to herself,

"Yeah, they probably just feel sorry for me." If she struggled with an assignment in school, her negative mind would say, "You'll never make it, those Jerks were right, you're defective in every way." One tool we used to combat these negative thoughts was to have her talk back to the thoughts, to re-frame the thoughts in a more optimistic way. Here are some examples of how Jessica would practice talking back to the negative mind processor:

Jessica's Thoughts	Jessica's Reframe
I can't do a good job in my education practicum.	If I keep practicing, I know I will learn it well enough to teach well.
My mentor must think I'm stupid.	I'm not a mind reader, I don't know what she thinks, but I can ask if I've upset her and maybe apologize.
My lesson was horrible.	Some lessons go better than others. I want to improve and that is good.
I'll never make it.	I've made it so far. All I have to do right now is what is in front of me, one step at a time.

It took some time, but eventually, Jessica got better at challenging the negative mind processor. She got better at letting go of what she couldn't control and focusing on things she could do something about. Part of her re-frame was also getting her to focus on the things she did well, and to avoid comparing herself to others. Some of the fixed or stuck thought pathways of her mind were to over-focus on her weaknesses and failures. She was getting better at spotting and avoiding Jerks, but she would beat herself up mercilessly for her dating mistakes of the past. To combat this, we would focus on what she did well, we practiced positive self-talk, and we gave her credit when she did hard things or did things she didn't really enjoy. Sometimes, Jessica would get overwhelmed because she would expect perfection (something she learned from her mother). We worked on changing her expectations and made plans to get back on track when she would have a bad day—a big part of getting back on track was reminding her often of why she wanted to change.

After dedicated effort, Jessica was able to change her brain connections. She graduated from college and easily was able to get a teaching position in the local school district. The real test came when she started dating Rick. From the start, she made sure to voice her own thoughts and opinions and not fear what he thought. At first, she overcompensated by being downright bossy about what she wanted to do on dates and was extra sensitive at any hint of Jerkness. Rick was patient and persistent. She learned to trust him, and was able to break free of the need to please him. There was no drama or desperation in the relationship like with previous Jerks. Her confidence increased in her ability to make good choices. If they ever got in an argument and Rick was unhappy about the situation, she wouldn't interpret his unhappiness as rejection. She instead tried to see his perspective, and made sure she was clear about her point of view. She was able to compartmentalize the issue without making it a global issue that previously led to her feeling abandoned, insecure, and alone.

Another key issue in her ability to demagnetize was having appropriate boundaries with her parents, especially her mother. I actually had to work with her mother individually to educate her on how she enabled and rescued Jessica. Her mother didn't understand how she subtly treated Jessica like she was incapable of being successful on her own. Her mother had to be taught not to make Jessica feel guilty for not performing at the highest level. Even though Jessica was an adult, her mother needed help in encouraging and rewarding Jessica's process rather than her outcome. Most importantly, Jessica had to stop putting so much emphasis on her mother's approval, and her mother had to stop doling out advice for every situation. This process took time, but eventually Jessica gained confidence in her abilities and felt more independent, which translated to an ability to have a healthy relationship with her mother and Rick.

So, to review and sum up:

1.   Like a magnet, you are filled with tiny individual experiences that work together to shape you into the person you are.

2. You have within you Charged Particles or stuff that happens or has happened during your life that shapes your self-esteem and view of the world. These are the memorable trail markers along your life path—the things you use to define yourself.

3. The Charged Particles can contribute to Electric Currents or ingrained patterns of thought, feeling, or behavior that cause Jerks to be attracted to you and you to them.

4. The Charged Particles and Electric Currents can create powerful attractive forces between two people, also known as Magnetic Fields.

5. By taking the two Jerk Tests and the Abuse Test, you should be able to identify Players—mild charmers who use you and undermine your confidence and *Mean*ipulators—controllers and abusers.

6. You should also be aware of the existence and tactics of South Pole Psychopaths, be able to get their history, recognize their lies, and run away.

7. You can understand the mysteries of becoming a Jerk Magnet, the basics of child and adolescent development, the pitfalls of the people pleaser, the dynamics of the drama triangle, and the features of personalities, specifically the Dependent Personality Disorder.

8. You can demagnetize by doing more than just think differently; you have to behave differently. Do things that you haven't always done. Challenge the automatic thoughts you have about yourself.

9. Parents can identify Jerk Magnet traits early in brain development and "nip them in the bud" in order to help their child own their emotions, understand natural consequences of behavior, and get fulfillment from the process rather than the outcome.

10. Application of these principles will cause neural pathways to change due to changes in behavior, environment, thinking, and emotions. New connections will help you reframe the automatic negative thoughts, and ultimately help you to resist the attraction of Jerks and eventually be demagnetized forever.

The changes that can happen are real. It was exciting to work with Jessica and her family to help them understand the forces acting upon their life. Although I have highlighted Jessica's story throughout this book, I have worked with hundreds of similar people and family systems that similarly needed to see how their Charged Particles contributed to the Electric Currents of repeating negative unhealthy relationships. The principles of the book, if applied, really can help you recognize the root of the problem and overcome the personality patterns that cause attraction to Jerks. It takes patience and time, but you can do it.

National Domestic Violence Hotline
1-800-799-SAFE(7233)
Available: 24/7, 365 days a year. Bilingual advocates on hand
Resource: thehotline.org
Chat now: M-F, 10am-8pm, Eastern Standard Time

National Resource Center on Domestic Violence
nrcdv.org
An agency providing comprehensive information for those
wanting to educate themselves and help others on the many
issues related to domestic violence.

Runaway & Homeless Youth and Relationship Violence Toolkit
Nrcdv.org/rhydvtoolkit
Enhancing the safety and healing of young people living
situations marked by violence and abuse.

Center for Relationship Abuse Awareness
stoprelationshipabuse.org
The mission of the Center for Relationship Abuse Awareness is
to educate communities, institutions, and young leaders to
take collective action against gender violence.

Teen Dating Violence, Intimate Partner Violence Information
www.cdc.gov/ViolencePrevention/
intimatepartnerviolence/teen_dating_violence.html
Center for Disease Control and Prevention (CDC) website

Dating Abuse Statistics
www.loveisrespect.org
Loveisrespect is the ultimate resource to empower youth to
prevent and end dating abuse. It is a project of Break the Cycle
and the National Domestic Violence Hotline.

Band Back Together
 bandbacktogether.com/emotional-abuse-resources
 Emotional Abuse Resource. Emotional Abuse is when the
 perpetrator uses fear, humiliation, or verbal assault to
 undermine the self-esteem of their victim.

Respect Love, Love Respect
 Respectlove.opdv.ny.gov/resources/index.html
 Resources to deal with dating abuse, including resources for
 schools and information about public awareness campaigns.

**U.S. Department of Health & Human Services—Office of
Adolescent Health.**
 www.hhs.gov/ash/oah/resources-and-publications/
 publications/healthy-relationships.html
 The Office of Adolescent Health has identified a comprehensive
 range of federal resources on adolescent health relationships.

Women Against Abuse
 Womenagainstabuse.org
 Whether you are in an abusive relationship, or if you are worried
 about a friend, these resources can help you get the information
 you need.

Violence Against Women
 womenshealth.gov/violence-against-women/types-of-violence
 Information regarding dating violence and how to get help.

SafeTeens
 Safeteens.org/relationships
 SafeTeens has guides for understanding many common teen
 relationship problems, tips for handling difficult situations, and
 resources to get more help.

Relationship Articles
 psychcentral.com/resources/Relationship/Articles/
 Collection of Top Rated Articles on relationship problems,
 self-tests and resources related to having a maintaining a health
 relationship.